Swimming
Toward the Sun

Collected Poems: 1968-2020

ESSENTIAL POETS SERIES 279

Guernica Editions Inc. acknowledges the support
of the Canada Council for the Arts and the Ontario Arts Council.
The Ontario Arts Council is an agency of the Government of Ontario.
We acknowledge the financial support of the Government of Canada.

Laurence Hutchman

Swimming Toward the Sun

Collected Poems: 1968-2020

GUERNICA
EDITIONS

TORONTO • CHICAGO • BUFFALO • LANCASTER (U.K.)
2020

Michael Mirolla, general editor
Eva Kolacz, editor
Cover and Interior Design: Rafael Chimicatti
Cover Image: Sean Hutchman
Guernica Editions Inc.
287 Templemead Drive, Hamilton (ON), Canada L8W 2W4
2250 Military Road, Tonawanda, N.Y. 14150-6000 U.S.A.
www.guernicaeditions.com

Distributors:
Independent Publishers Group (IPG)
600 North Pulaski Road, Chicago IL 60624
University of Toronto Press Distribution (UTP),
5201 Dufferin Street, Toronto (ON), Canada M3H 5T8
Gazelle Book Services, White Cross Mills
High Town, Lancaster LA1 4XS U.K.

First edition.
Printed in Canada.

Legal Deposit – Third Quarter
Library of Congress Catalog Card Number: 2019912940
Library and Archives Canada Cataloguing in Publication
Title: Swimming toward the sun : collected poems 1968-2020 /
Laurence Hutchman.
Other titles: Poems
Names: Hutchman, Laurence, author.
Series: Essential poets ; 279.
Description: First edition. | Series statement: Essential poets series ; 279
Identifiers: Canadiana 20190176202 | ISBN 9781771835404 (softcover)
Classification: LCC PS8565.U83 A6 2020 | DDC C811/.54—dc23

Contents

Emery (1998)

Personal Encounters (2014)

Two Maps of Emery (2016)

The House of Shifting Time (2019)

Fire and Water (2020)

For Eva as always,
and
Sean, Emma and Patty

the sun begins to break
the horizon. I swim toward it
as it sends golden rays across
the waves ...

"Swimming Toward the Sun"

Introduction

Song in the Vanished Places:
The Poetry of Laurence Hutchman

Laurence Hutchman is a uniquely Canadian poet in the best sense of the word. Yet he is undeservedly overlooked when Canadian poets are discussed because he has dared to write beyond the norms for what passes for poetry in this country. He is not a poet who revels in shock or writes about contemporary hot-button topics or, for that matter, someone who is part of the "in-crowd" that dominates the poetry scene. Those works that speak merely to the moment come and go from the Canadian poetry scene with startling brevity and frequency. I could name (but won't) poets who were the toast of the town forty, fifty years ago and whose works are long forgotten. The American poet, Jack Gilbert, defines courage as "the normal excellence of long accomplishment," and that is the case with Laurence Hutchman who is the best kind of poet, to my mind. He is a poet who writes carefully crafted poetry that stands up to the test of time. This book, a selection of his work over a fifty year span, is proof of my assertion.

In Hutchman's career of more than fifty years there is much to admire. I admired and published his poetry long before we met at the launch of my first book of poems at Irene McGuire's Toronto book-shop, Writers and Company, on March 25, 1988. Over the decades, Hutchman has moved from coast to coast and his work expresses a rare pan-Canadian experience. And whether he has been out west or down east, abroad or at home, we have kept in touch. When we meet there is always something to talk about, poetry the most important item, and our conversation picks up where it left off as if we are continuing, unbroken, a long, narrative song.

His poems have staying power, and they will be as true and re-flective of a master craftsman fifty years from now as they are today. His voice is rooted, imaginatively and almost spiritually, in the place where he grew up.

In a literature that is constantly being weakened critically and artistically by momentary voices whose importance fade almost the moment the ink hits the page, Hutchman's work carries many of the hallmarks of poetry that has survived the test of time – the love of nature expressed by Bliss Carman, the keen eye for observation articulated by Archibald Lampman, the gift of connecting the idea to the place found in Raymond Knister's opus, and the deep, energetic passion of Gwendolyn MacEwen's haunting lyricism. There is an echo in Hutchman's voice of Al Purdy, a poet he admires greatly and names as one of his key mentors. But I would argue that Hutchman captures the unique qualities of Purdy's poetry in a very different way. Purdy states the thing; Hutchman sings it. Poetry and song, in an age that revels in word play but dismisses the musicality of language as an antique notion, need to be seen as inseparable. The voice of the poet is still, and always will be, the voice of a singer who sits down and tells a story that is both accessible and melodically entertaining.

Several years ago when I was in New York City to give a reading in Bryant Park, Paul Romero – he who masterminded New York Fashion Week and who was the keeper of that city's marvellous public space behind the New York Public Library – hosted four Canadian poets for the afternoon. Romero, a keen, non-Canadian observer, said that three of the poets possessed what to his ear was "the uniquely Canadian voice." I was the exception. When I pressed him on the matter he couldn't define what he meant. But listening to the poetry of Laurence Hutchman, I am certain I hear what Romero heard in my work and that is the element of song that cannot be learned but that arises from a mixture of place, background, and theme. In part, Hutchman's work owes an acknowledgement to the Irish bardic tradition that is part of his heritage. But there is something more about his voice that haunts me because it is the song of his place on the earth, just as Al Purdy's poetry was inseparable from his experience in Ontario's Prince Edward County.

The "uniquely Canadian voice" that Romero said he heard plays with silence. The voice seeks silence. Often, it gaps. To my ear, it is as flat as someone announcing that the next train to somewhere is delayed. It ponders the line that drops at its end rather than lilts melodically into the next phrase or statement. Perhaps this lilt is cadence, though there is something more ingrained in Hutchman's ear than a mere rising and falling of the voice as a result of inflexion. The lilt in Hutchman's voice is informed by two sources that have shaped his life.

When I hear Laurence Hutchman read, and we have read together many times, I realize we both sprang from similar roots planted firmly in the Celtic lilt and in the experience of a lost rural Canada being transformed into a crowded metropolis. His words pour like water off the tongue. His lines do not state as much as they intone. In his early work, Hutchman tackled Celtic subjects. Returning to Ireland when he was twenty, just before the beginning of the Troubles, he witnessed riots in Derry. When he writes about grief he keens. When he writes about joy or love, even in his recent and exquisitely touching poems to his wife Eva, he sings with grand eloquence that is muted, constrained, and focussed in what Dante would call "the Illustrious" voice of tragic language and hymnal praise. This quality of language is not just a matter of having a good ear. This is the voice of someone who has sprung from a tradition that cannot be ignored for the sake of conforming to a dictum of what constitutes a "national voice." Hutchman's poems contain that element that Paul Romero could not name in mine. It is the passion for one's subject matter that drives a poet beyond merely saying something and into the realm of singing about it. I admire him greatly for the fact that he has embraced Romero's unnamed element and put it to good use.

The second informing agent in Hutchman's poetry is place. As a boy growing up in Emery, Ontario, one of the many rural villages that were swallowed by the burgeoning boundaries of Toronto, Hutchman understood the place where he lived, what the Irish would term the *dinnseanchas* tradition – the voice and spirit of the place that cannot be taken out of a location. The Irish playwright, Brian Friel, has a play about this concept, *Translations*, where he the dramaturge argues that the meaning of the land cannot be taken out of the geography and forever plays an active role of informing everything that springs from a landscape. I see this at work in Hutchman's poems of Emery because I experienced it in my own work. I grew up in what had been Oriole, another of the lost villages that were consumed by the subdivisions of North York and eventually the City of Toronto and then the GTA.

Hutchman possesses a double-vision that is all too familiar to me. He sees Emery not only for what it is now but for what it was. He traces the ghostly outlines of the last of the early nineteenth century houses and churches and graveyards torn up, buried, and trampled by expansion. Irish and Scottish poetry, the poetry of Seamus Heaney and Hugh

McDiarmid, sees the world through this double-vision, and laments what is gone by celebrating what remains. McDiarmid's "Island Funeral," for example, describes the delicate turnings of a handcrafted chair in a crofter's cottage in the same way that Hutchman offers us his version of that double-vision in "Two Maps of Emery:"

> Look at the lines on the map,
> how they lead beyond the page
> into the fields and orchards I knew,
> to barbed wire fences that I climbed.

It would be easy enough to say that Hutchman is giving his familiar territory the "Al Purdy treatment," a fathoming of the past. But where Purdy, in his Ameliasburgh poems, is an archaeologist of the past, digging down through layers of dirt (as Heaney does in the poems of the first half of his career), Hutchman is a diviner who talks to the dead because their spirits are still very alive in the places they knew.

Throughout his career, Hutchman has embraced a number of landscapes. A reader of this volume might argue that he is a New Brunswick poet, a voice defined by the places he lived and wrote about. His poems of his travels are perceptive, eloquent, and offer wonderful paeans to wherever he has been, but they lack the haunting spirit of Emery, and like a ghost who cannot leave what he has loved and presumably lost, he keeps returning to the place that shaped his vision because his most profound passions spring from it:

> Look at the buildings on the map
> drawn by Marion Rowntree in the 1940s:
> the blacksmith shop, the carriage shop,
> the shingle mill, the community hall
>
> ....
>
> Who are these farmers that ploughed the fields,
> their tractors navigating the warm sea of wheat?
> Who are the soldiers whose names are
> engraved on the monument?
> What stories are hidden under the fading lines of this stone?

....

For years I've been away,
yet their houses have haunted my dreams.
The farmers' voices said, "Turn from your work.
Return to a place that is no longer there."
I dream of a clear river that flows through Emery,
of a tree that grows through school windows.
"Journey," say the voices, "to find your history.
Here is the place you are looking for."

As Purdy puts it in his poem, "The Country North of Belleville":

sometime
we may go back there
                    to the country of our defeat

....

But it's been a long time since
And we must enquire the way
            of strangers –

What Laurence Hutchman achieves, whether in his Emery poems
or in the poetry of the places that he has discovered and where he has
discovered himself, is a roadmap through time that offers not merely
a glimpse of what is or was, but a song, a means of committing life to
memory, that invites the reader to listen and join in.

Bruce Meyer

The Twilight Kingdom
(1973)

A Still Field

The sun particles burst
over the violet horizon,
illuminate darker aspects of the field.

We walk through the arcade of elm,
black branches hang over rubbish,
yellow faded deaths of yesterday afternoon.

The flowers grow through the rocks—
this is the world each one of us lives in,
regardless of the theories of the day.

Perseus

The stain on the ceiling
assumes tremendous energy.
Perseus on a white steed
glides over dim Attic coasts,
light on the Dorian pillars.

Down from the pines of Pelion
the mane of Pegasus flows against the stars.
Riding through night
into the white storm of violence,
the large rider's sword is burnished
against its flank under the silver moon.
Hooves move silently on the glowing air;
the high shoulders, sleek tense arms
will slay the dragon soon.

Perseus rides off the ceiling,
but the old lady who lived here before
saw the shape of the stain
as the incarnate fear of her dead husband.

Lifeguard

The bricks have never been so red.
The sky is blue as it was in the beginning—
a clear pastel eternity.
The clouds are fantastic swirls, feelings.
The brilliant grass glimmers through the fence,
and I must watch this lonely swimmer,
ten years old and struggling in the shallow water.
"Look, I can almost touch the bottom."

"Go away, I want to be with Rilke.
Go away and leave me alone with the sky."
He is panting, gurgling, laughing, asking questions,
then breaks the surface with a frightened stare.

There the clouds, fence, trees and red bricks.
"Go away, I want to be with Rilke."
I look at him in the water.
I am looking at Rilke.

Greenisland, Belfast

The people had an ancient charm
but in their voice was pain—
sad movement of the village air
born out of the harbour fog.

Past the old schoolhouse
children's voices echo in the wood
and over the green and yellow hillside
the sunlight wavers on far Belfast.

The black cenotaph stands against the grey sea
over the place where I was born.
The white dung dries on the letters,
a forgotten love through closed eyes.

I walk down the empty road
by woods and streams and farms;
then the wind suddenly changes.
I turn away from the black sign of war.

The Girl and the Fisherman

A time for pleasure comes,
orange letters open out of darkness.
Away from the party, she moves down rocky slopes,
among the debris and the fisherman's secret.

And he ties the net,
mumbling worn words
as tight as the wind's edges.
His body is haggard under a thin coarse beard.

At the party there were no secrets.
The woman on the beach raises her fingers
away from the waves on the sand,
trying to form an anguished cause out of the tide.

And the fisherman's secret:
slowly he pulls the net
over the ribbed sand at her delicate feet.
The mist drifts over the house, and the sea is clear.

Vigil

Love,
we talk night and day
care not to sleep
sun pours over rock
we merge in ecstasy
and in the violet void
from sun through moon
we ebb in tide to rest.

The Solitary Scales

The regret of evening lingers red
over the rim of this unquiet world.
The black crow flies by night
over the white watch of the moon
as I walk past the cathedral,

down the blind alleys
where the lights are dim, curtains drawn
and my thoughts rise over glimmering canals
away from the conforming lovers
to the lonely sparkles of the void.

At midnight in the stillness
the music slowly comes
from of all these people around me:
our care and indifference
measured in the blind scales of ivory stars.

New Year's Party

Restless I wander outdoors.
Over the snow bank by the fence
stars purple and white
are standing in twinkling silence.

The river cuts the hills of snow
and wind in the pines
ripples through the rock
vertigo, and then peace.

In the moon under chandeliers
dancing couples we don't know
talking of dead romantics,
frozen faces of a courtroom comedy.
The star of Christmas fading—
the uncertain light of the new year.

Explorations
(1975)

Explorations

for Les Kelly

In class when I was twelve
I traced different voyages,
travelled pale encyclopaedic seas:
Magellan round Cape Horn,
Livingstone into the dark continent.

Scott in Antarctica,
thousands of miles from home
where no man had ever been
was dying for the purity of exploration;
his candle expired on the eternal snow plain.

After school each day became an exploration,
the moment always changing.
The teacher never understood
the logic of our search;
the countryside was our classroom,
and the current of the Humber river
breaking the silence of the earth.

Somewhere in Africa is the missing bone.
And earlier the red meteor flashed,
spinning down through the primordial night,
down through Ungava's murky skies.
Still earlier, the crystal
is born of the first fire on the black earth.

St. Patrick's Cemetery

Slowly through the black gate he walks
into the shadow of the leaning tombs.
Music of the sea-wind in the trees
blows through the sparkling grass.
He holds the flowers tightly,
places them on his silent mother's grave.
Beyond him rise the lovely mountains of Mourne.

Film in Paris

After tipping the usher
we sat down,
listened to the newscaster:
Londonderry, August, 1969.
Beyond the dark heads
petrol bombs explode on the screen.

Months earlier, I was in Ireland
ten thousand Catholics
broke the police cordon,
battled the Protestant crowd.

The reporters lied.
The crowds smashed cameras
just as in this newsreel.

Now it's safely history.
We settle back and watch
Once Upon a Time in the West

Outside, the sun bristles the leaves
and workers are drilling
under the Arc de Triomphe.

Passage

Beyond my still reflection
grey road curves into night,
gold leaves fall
and the wind moans
as dark thin needles of the pine
shroud the moon's full face
and pale rays fall
over church, highway and open fields.

By the Pool

Let us dive now, love
into the pool where reflections of parasols
convey our aqua illusions,
where the water
blurs our soft enfolding bodies.

Let us dive now into the river
through the pebbles and over the falls,
by rusty cans and strange sirens
and through the razor rain
to love under the lips of open leaves.

The sun is born in the east
and on this Mediterranean terrace
there is only one way
through the mountain pass—
that secret valley.

Fog Over Mount Royal

There are bars across the window
and we are isolated,
live with our separate illusions
in the comfort of this room.

We leave the apartment
walk slowly up Mount Royal,
trees gnarled against the hospital,
guards before an embassy recently bombed.

Then the steps through dirty snow:
a few dogs, birds, children,
noises in the mist.
As we climb, the view disappears.

At the top we are alone
in this still greyness.
Through the black trees
there is no world.

Fog drifts over the chalet
our steps echo on silent floors.
Under pastel pictures of Quebec's history
an old man is talking about survival.

The Hockey Game

Before the face-off
of the Toronto-Montreal game
he begins talking:

—Yes, I have been here a few years.
You know I am Polish ... After the war
I spent five years in Siberia.

—It was below zero in winter.
We had to cut wood in the daytime.
At night we slept in tents.

—I was strong then;
now I feel the pain in my shoulders.
When you are young it doesn't ...

—Because I told the truth,
some normal thing in conversation,
I was taken away.

Ice shines brightly on his glasses;
players flash across his vision
through red circles and blue lines.

—I am an optometrist now.

He smiles, cheers
for a good game.

The Boxer

We leave the Miramichi Hotel,
walk through Newcastle's town square
past Lord Beaverbrook's smug bust,
his gazebo, his Italian sundial.
In the harbour a warship is docked.

Outside of town we hitchhike.
A yellow car stops.
The driver introduces himself as Yvon,
says that he used to box.

I remember him well,
from the Friday night fights
I watched with my father.
When he fought Archie Moore
for the world championship,
he knocked him down again and again
and still lost.

"I fought all over the world:
England, South Africa, Russia.
It's a racket … I retired in 1960.
I owed the government 45,000 dollars.
Paid them off last year."

"The best fight … I fought was with a South African—
lost three teeth, had my nose broken,
my chest busted."
He rubs my fingers over his ribs.
" I won that fight, knocked him out in the eighth.
Don't know how I survived."

The Chinese Man

In the afternoon
the old Chinese man
kneels in a garden.

The sunlight flickers—
a golden tapestry on the red wall.

Jazz from an old film echoes;
a broken leaf falls.

He feels for a single nail,
sets it on the wood,
hammers straight as thought.

Resolute he is,
the golden tapestry on the red wall.

Mozart in the Supermarket

Here is a superabundance of food:
chocolate ants from Africa,
bananas from South America,
a thousand oranges from California.
We wind our way among these stands,
the music reeling around our heads.

We are confronted with richness of goods,
yet the subtle emptiness everywhere.
We stand before the clanging registers,
the shopping carts filled with packages,
loud newscasters between commercials.
A language everyone consumes, but few digest.

The centre of the world is everywhere,
and when I hold these goods
the music returns:
the moment's sudden clear harmony,
Star of Venus in the blue dawn.

The Highway

1. London

Past Victoria Park
skaters glide before the canons.
Down Richmond to Wellington Road
round the ramp onto the highway we drive,
away from winter's imperial absolute.
Clouds streak grey against the cold sun.

Before us is the map
of small towns with big names:
Zurich, Paris, Vienna, London.
We follow this journey through the white land.

Wind drifts through deserted barns,
across bleak fields, coloured silos.
The wide silent Grand sweeps on,
crystals dazzle by dark banks
along these shores,
dead trees, long forgotten wars.

Workers bulldoze the smoky forests,
the animals now are gone.
Below the hillside, round the curve we travel.
Leisure Lodge glimmers through the pines
in the oncoming headlamps of the future.

Star spangled sky over red-domed station,
Kandinsky's lines in the constellation,
silver rays of native thought
fleck the land's rough slate.
We drive life elsewhere.

Moon is a polished stone
hanging on dark escarpment.
Mist, a silvery garment
enfolds skiers of the night.

2. Toronto

Metaphysical City:
buildings darken the horizon,
rivers flow to harbour isles.
Fine names on the subway:
Davisville, Summerhill, Rosedale.
Between their yellow stations
stands Mt. Pleasant with its gravestones.
Below Bloor, the saints—George, Patrick, Andrew—
go underground.

On Yonge Street:
old men preach about their souls,
young men gaze at the female flesh,
intellectuals scan bookracks.

Between Philosopher's Walk and Queen's Park
we glide; hippies and revolutionaries
surround the conquered Edward VII,
away from the university and brown Parliament.

Downtown business highlights:
the yellow beams of accidents,
the violet sparks of the trams.
Smoke drifts across the bank towers,
skaters glide before *The Archer*.
At the library of City Hall
I read the *Original Wasteland* and McLuhan.

Around us Toronto breathes
through a thin used gauze.
And time curves, bends
from space to place
back to land again.
Digital clocks will straighten us out.

3. The Land

The land seems empty.
Sunlight gleams on the shelf of water
when we drive between blue hills
farther into the glowing emptiness.

Dim sun glows in misty valleys—
Hurons, Algonquins, Mohawks
perished by musket and disease.
We have not loved the land.

Away from courts of the old world
first voyageurs canoed swift river,
deeper into the forest
in search of animals.
New worlds sparkled on white water.
Static between sermons and hockey scores
as clouds roll down the luminous sky
Abraham, Waterloo, Versailles ...

WORDS

Our senses fuse under heavy skies
Gold light flashes into still eyes.

On windy fields.
Americans ... English ... Canadians ... Aboriginals
slain
        no manifest destiny.

Nous arrivons au Québec
au nord, les villages,
les panneaux rouges
contre les Laurentides violettes,
les îlots de pins flottants
sur les grands lacs.
Ici se trouvent les nouvelles langues.

L'art et la ville
nos aventures et nos morts.
We wind our way along this paved path
by construction crews, new linguists
who wave red flags to foreign motorists.

4. Montreal

We accelerate again
  move down these arteries
dream in a single direction
   down
       into
           the vortex:

            TOSHIBA

GOODYEAR   KRAFT

   SALADA   LA BELLE FERMIÈRE

We pass Westmount's calm stone mansions,
drive quickly along Côte-des-Neiges,
down the Sherbrooke corridor.
Cranes turn their heads, drills echo.
Les ruelles sont muettes.

In downtown the jewels sparkle in dark windows
against the green and tarnished statues.
Sunlight falls on the mingling crowd,
pigeons rise through flickering shadows
across Ville Marie's silver artifice.

We walk toward the mountain
past restaurants, stores, universities.
The wind echoes a crystal song
and the sleek white limbs of birch
affirm an older spirit of the land.

Wind brings a deeper force,
brilliant rays flash into our vision,
and on the blue-gold horizon
the Saint Lawrence glimmers,
flowing out toward the world.

Pictures from an Exhibition

Eternal chimes,
chimes of the world,
chimes of the stars—
here in the glass case
three languages describe ruins.

We enter the exhibition slowly—
the first craniums, the tools,
the sculpted green bowl.
It is not a ford.
The green bowl is becoming a person.

Now in the glass case
the tools, the craniums
look out at us.
We are prisoners in a museum.
We are behind glass,
reading lies, archaeological labels.

Here we feel the sweep of the wind
seven centuries before Christ.
The young girl looks through glass,
a girl seven centuries before Christ,
looks up with clear eyes into the rain
and here the chimes … the chimes …

People: Indian, Chinese, French, German, Canadian
move beyond symbols: horse, leopard, soldier, queen
the chimes … the chimes …
the wind, the rain, the girl.

At the end of the hall
another bowl glows.
We look into the luminous centre
then move on
     through
          chimes

     chimes   *chimes*

       chimes

Expectation

Red light flashes against the mountain.
    The moment is absurd
patterns are unassuming,
                  not involved
          nor involving
but something is about to happen,
                    any moment.

Wreckers pull walls down.
    Unexpected voices in the wind
drift past newsstands
            with pretty naked girls,
                black headlines of murder.
              Neon lights in grey space.

Wind howls through the ruins
        past monuments, churches, skyscrapers
           past the large windows
where young secretaries dream.

We feel
    the subtle senses
tighten, bend,
    allowing the corners of the world in.
All around the city
    people at their windows
                watching
          waiting.

Blue Riders
(1985)

Saint Columba

Exiled by clerics you turn
from the green lonely hills
where your oak trees grew in the nourishing mist
and you see the world's pattern in the raven's flight,
high beyond Grianan's pagan walls.
The hand of God guides you
along the craggy shores of Inishowen,
and the devil's currents lash your bark.

Your destiny is a shining lamp,
your words rise through mist.
Your guide is the coracle
out of Lough Foyle into the Irish Sea.
Anger distills in your heart.

The laws are strict in a time of darkness
when barbarian hordes ride
to Europe's edge: you keep
the lamp burning low as you write sacred scrolls,
counsel your secular monks
to watch for the injured bird.

And could you, Columba, return now
to your oak grove to see how the clerics
and bitter men of politics
have armed the population—
then you would know how they
have scarred your Ireland.

Three Houses

Near this country's border
a white road winds among green hills.
A cottage is joined to a larger house.
The gardener digs his plot,
ravens caw to crude gods,
water gurgles from a rusty pipe.

On the hilltop
the surgeon's house is quiet
beyond the trees and holly bushes.
One night on the Antrim Road
his son is shot dead from a speeding car.

Now inside in an abandoned house,
curtains decay on broken frames,
whiskey moulders in boxes marked by royal lions,
a faded calendar hangs from before the war.
"Who's coming around the bend?"
Only two cyclists and a whistling boy,
human cries echoing in the wind.

Music in the Snow

Now is the moment when things fit:
    the bankbook drops into a secret pocket,
    money again, and the boundary comes clear
    under a halo of the light bulb.

This is the moment, the resumption of music
    when the moon parts her curtain,
    and logic is a fence following
    the slope of hills.

Now is the moment, the striking of the baton,
    twirling of gold coins on counters,
    meeting of lips.
    Here one will dance on snow,
    not act on the tragic stage.

This is the moment when
    the picture lifts out of the canvas,
    swirls back deeply into the cosmos
    of the creator's heart,
    the strong rush by semilunar valves—
    love you moon of my heart, my heart.

Girl Walking on Friday Afternoon

Over the sidewalk she moves,
her dark coat above her hips.

She does not alter her pace
under the myths in stained glass
the gothic domes.

She glides
through melting snow
toward mountain boulevard.

She stoops, turns,
raises three curled fingers
to the strands of her hair,
glances into the bright wind.

Josie of Flower Street

The steamy room where Father drank
and sisters swarmed around me.
Mornings the odour of bad meat
hung in the air. Afternoons
brought the sick smell of steam
rising from filthy clothes.

That night when the Dane approached me,
thrusting more money into my hand
than I made in a week at the laundry,
I bought my first red dress.

When the sea wind drifted into the city,
sailors from all over the world
would come and want me then.
I was young, tawny
not one of those caged birds for tourists.
My leg hurts again. It's raining,
but not as it did that night
when the car beams blinded me.
Emergency, the priest
blessed with the dangling cross
digging his fingers into my thighs.

There are not so many men now.
That morning, the client was slowly
undressing, taking his socks
off last, pressing his fingers
into my back, trying to get
hold of something.
Then his cheeks flushed red
as he arched into shock,
his eyes cold as the room
around me.

I was in my dressing gown
when the police came.
I couldn't answer their simple questions,
just kept smoking, looking down
into the grave of the garden.

You Should Always Carry a Pen

I look out of the library
window into the blue city;
my reflection sails over
silver buildings,
up to the billows of smoke.

And the words come easily
in the interior of this building,
luminous rooms of your mind.

Beside me the woman operates
the Xerox, amazing x-ray machine
turning the sky phosphorescent.
She, the temptress in green,
transforms the evening
into a blue ocean myth.

You should always carry a pen,
especially at twilight,
if you are to believe
the memoirs of Coleridge,
his nightly walks by misty lakes.
The woman slips the pages of her book
into an envelope
                and disappears.

I take the *Eagle Mirado*,
    ride the lines of flight
        over the darkening city.

Two Oranges

Snow hangs on the fence;
the air is cold blue,
death a dark window.

I am learning to feel.
Before me two oranges
in a brown bowl.

I hold them,
feel their weight rise
through my fingers into my arms.

In this silence before sleep
I place two oranges
within the rim of our lives.

Pinballs

Under fingertips machine music
    moves to your inner rhythm;
       the ball springs into an arc,
slides down fortune's alley,
        spins through the gates
of paradise
           past pyramids
    tempting sirens
pillars of Hercules
      the liberty bell
    into a space odyssey.
Dexterity is your art.
    You are musician, soldier, lover
in this world of light, action.
     You press, flick, gyrate
and the silver ball
      contacts the coloured points.
Among grey-haired businessmen,
     expert boys and savvy girls
you combat the machine
    following the movement
of your fortune
    as the machine
        lights up your dream:
immersed you in coloured
    synaesthesia
           "Game Over."

Gourds

Weird fruit, you appear in golden baskets:
your skin moulded for Thanksgiving rituals,
noses bulbous as Rembrandt's bachelors,
curves full as Goya's dancing ladies.
Comedians of fruit, you
accept your imperfections as strength,
chuckle form carbuncular cheeks.
And when all others have exited
you are autumn's exotic personalities,
laughing through your Hallowe'en masks.
You are weird, wonderful creatures,
veteran poets content to be yourselves
in spite of the world.

Balcony

Glancing for the number of your house on Sainte-Famille,
I pass these Parisian fronts with Brooklyn railings,
Sherbrooke's tarnished figures from antiquity.

On the door glass a pastel flower
blooms:
I bound up the stairs
as they give way, waves
leap into the light of your apartment,
music of Morocco swirling
through Greek pillars, crystal chandeliers,
a mosque glimmering in dark water;
in the alcove people are waiting.

You, on the balcony by a rusty railing
wait: pigeons, grey-mauve, green feathers
rise through heat
vertigo.
We sit on this shaky balcony
above Sainte-Famille
talking about Indian rhythms, black rhythms.
One floor down
a girl in blue garb
sits at her round red table
café, fromage et croissants.

Soon in the yellow kitchen
the lady and the unicorn sing
of Mallarmé's angel;
     out there
     the lavender light
     the sun setting on the green mountain
     our dark bodies outlined
     the balcony
     glowing.

Nymphae

In the Botanical Gardens
pale women and men stroll
among the blossoming flowers
of the water-lily.
In French you are *Le Nénuphar*,
a Pre-Raphaelite Ophelia,
a yellow butterfly I saw once
on a stamp of Mozambique.
But in Greek, lady, you're my flower,
bride of water, amphibious beauty
whose fibrous body grows
down through those depths
                    into the earth.

What tragedy have you blossomed from?
You sang from the Delphic wood
the destiny of lonely women;
you appeared to metaphysical poets
in late English nights,
attracted Monet
who spent his final years
painting your body of petals.

Cool air wafts the lacy willow
along the white path we walk
solitary in the dazzling summer air.
Drowsy lotus aroma
drifts to us in the wind.

The Mountain

We drive to St-Viateur where Hasidic Jews
stroll by steaming bagels,
Greeks eat souvlaki in rusty Fords
under Acropolis posters.
Old fishermen
toss candied octopus,
sky blue crab.

We glide down Park Avenue
past the mountain's autumn garment.
Workers have scrubbed the statues
of the politicians, the lions and the angel.
Angel, protector of language,
your wings rise from concrete,
fly before the mountain's smoky colours.

In the movie theatre
I watch the last credits on the screen
linger, listen to scraps of other people's lives.
The crowd moves beyond the film's music:
scenes of the mother drowning in the ocean,
the daughter's angry soliloquy.
Old people stare at the closing curtains.

Night's hunger gathers around the mountain,
drifting among the dark statues.
In a theatre shop window
a circus: ballet dancers, unicycles, clowns!
Pastel lakes, houses, women,
an artist smiling at an imaginary country.

The road winds through the day
as these images rise through me.
The seeds are released from white pods,
fiery pinwheels drift through the tall grass
turning high above the graves.

Down the mountain
  past the Acropolis
  and the sky blue crab
    the octopus
      the bursting milk pods
        past the angel
          the lions and the workers
          past the painter
          past graveyards
            churches
              theatres
                we drive.

I bite into the pomegranate,
remember this mountain path.

Nelligan

Getting off the metro on the way to work
I would see your face in that bronze
constellation with Garneau and Crémazie
as the crowd eddied on.
Your thought was the colour of distant moons.

Through years I have gathered the tableaux:
the house where you played on Carré Saint-Louis,
the old winding streets where you sauntered with Dantin,
the tortuous voyage to Liverpool and Belfast,
and that clear night at the Château Ramezay.

You left family and friends,
sailed to Belfast.
Out of the mist the brown shaded
city rose as the vessel glided
among skeletal cranes, prehistoric
creatures rising out of the ancestral land.

This was no golden vessel,
no Celtic world of green song;
among sailors you were a stranger.
At night the ship rolled
and the poems would come in dreams:
half-naked women wandering
among ruined naves, women
draped in nuns' habits,
shining bright as ravens' wings.

Again you move in your natal forest
and the purple mountains and green hills
where lecherous Capuchins revel
with the languorous women of Rubens.

Your thought was the colour of distant moons,
the white boat sailing
through the psychic darkness.

That night at the Château Ramezay
reading to the crowd,
your voice rose into song,
burst forth with night purity
for the beauty of women
by the gleaming leaves,
and the notes chimed
on the unknown scales
                              of the constellation.

And you, Émile,
you searched for pure beauty
gazed through words' violet radiation
toward the blazing mountain
until that night the songs
flooded your vessel
and you collapsed in fever.

Nietzsche saw the man whipping the horse
high up on the mountain;
the sun lashed the blister of the sea
and the moon's broken lute
sank under the waves.

One night I heard your poems
sung by the *chansonnière*
at *Le Patriote*, your face
in that of the young woman,
but above the shouting and laughing
to popular songs, the stamping
to an Irish jig and on her
invocation of your death,
you expired to Volare.

I walked toward the Hotel-Dieu,
stopped at a friend's on Jeanne-Mance,
listened to Brahms' "Requiem."
Thunder cracked the sky.
Two girls came to the door.
The one with glasses said,
"*Nous cherchons une chambre.*"
Her father was the *infirmier*
in whose arms you died.

The silence claimed you;
I walked home through mist.
Lamps glowed like eyes in the night
and the green shoots sprouted
through the cracked earth.

At Baudelaire's Grave

"Où est la tombe de Charles Baudelaire?"
The red nosed concierge laughs:
"La troisième pierre à gauche."
Jerks his thumb as though
directing me to a lost neighbour.

Your name engraved
beneath that of the disliked Aupic,
on a slate petals formed
by a child into a crown.

And the wind trembles in the leaves.
What is death?
On the path a black cat
winks a green eye.

In this graveyard
the old man, the flowers, the cat—
your symbols—
and there above the graveyard wall
                    les merveilleux nuages

After the Blizzard

Sweeping against the sky,
snow whirls around balconies;
grey clouds gather in the zenith
as the wind rises, beating the snow.
In the pool, girls laughing
as boys splash around,
skies darkening beyond the snow screen.

Someone is talking about apocalypse,
the swimmers gone, the pool now aquamarine.
Above the mount's black and white rim
touches of orange, yellow, rose.

In the blue sea of sky, white fish swim past
darker clouds, horsemen riding
the pathway of the evening
over the city
across the pastel meadow,
round the sapphire world.
Drifting deeper into night
we lie in bed.
Smoke drifts through darkness
a white beacon scans a starless sky
a door bangs—
someone steps into night.
The electric current of the orange clock
trills in rapids over pebbles.
A cat meows.
A child's plaintive cry is the wind
echoing through dark alleys.

In the Chinese pagoda a candle glimmers
burning its violet and yellow flame.
We are calm as the river.

Night View

Your voice is the wind
of late winter streets,
the breath of empty chalk-white roads.
Canticles of the mountain road
carry your silver metaphors
to the sky's icy rim,
sweep through chateaux,
past domed asylums and old lamps
to grey breaths murmuring,
under the cold blue exile of this night.

Blue Rider

My headlights penetrate mist.
Highway guides blind white land
into evening's frozen forms:
lost lakes, forest's snowy network,
starry coverts, unsurveyed fields—
Kandinsky's metaphors in code.

I follow these shifting lanes.
Blue Rider, you weave a blue-gold symphony
        from the Murnau Mountains,
        colour voices:
                yellows trumpets
                    violet bassoons
                        aqua flutes.
The frontiers of our pen chart
maps of nature's laws,
encompass the picture
not idea, but form itself.

A man without a country
        you trek roads of Russia
Europe and Africa
        ride by war-torn trenches
hungry refugees
        journals of death
                the burning of your paintings.

Towards form's unaccustomed continent you voyage
to enter a luminous genesis
of symmetry and planes.
Infinitesimal stars shimmer in a matrix sea.

You paint through time:
    pharaoh's journey
    sailor's odyssey
    spaceman's walk.
Ride the future
      into the universe of psyche:
         dream mandalas
              playful arabesques
         erotic alphabets
              capricious physiologies.

Ride the eye's horizon
where the cosmic kaleidoscope turns
countless starbursts
into lines of musical light
raining into
forests   lakes   fields.

Foreign National
(1993)

Dream of Origins

I wake up to see the headlines:
science has discovered God.
A scientist has probed and found
particles of radiation,
the origins of the universe rippling
on a distant primordial shore.
I look upon the blue and pink shell—
the genesis of all we know.
This morning in the elegant hotel room
the children, as usual, scramble over the bed.

I am always searching for the beginning:
in the stroller I'm watching the orange sky
suffused through black tangled branches;
in the playhouse I'm looking at the excited eyes
of birds, wondering how I am like them.

I dream of going back to Ireland after the war
to rescue Granny's relics.
Father said, "You should search the photos
to get the whole picture":
playing hockey with potato sack nets with Les,
the mad minister, the puritan boarders,
the old fishermen who returned,
the young soldiers who did not.

You cannot deny them.
You must take your family with you.
We are always looking for that beginning,
that first moment we mouth our names,
when we hear voices and know they are us,
when history comes out of the photos.
It is then we cry out against
bruised skin, blind vision.

It is then we travel through the dark morning,
gaze from the edge at the beginning:
in the distant sea of space,
and in the distant, intimate matrix,
the blue and pink celestial shell.

Lost Language

These photo albums span the decades:
wartime, marriage, early years in Canada.
The sounds of Dutch swell within me.

I read a language I knew and forgot—
"J's" and "T's" and Dutch diphthongs
(how ashamed I was of those comic vowels).
Sounds rise and break in me,
sibilance of sea, rush of waves
Scheveningen, Katwijk, Noordwijk ...

Sounds ripen in the mouth:
beschuit, pindakaas, boterham
sinaasappel ... lekker ... ah ... a language of violets,
orchids, solariums, and that tobacco ...

The words break in me.
Touching the page they dissolve the lines
of my mother's handwriting—
change into weather, the lonely
excitement of windy beaches,
seagrass, kelp, the briny smell
blowing the waking coldness off
Scheveningen, Katwijk, Noordwijk ...

The Park

1

That summer before we immigrated to Canada
we walked among tents at the market
where I ate *stroopwafels* and twirled a pinwheel.
Above Wassenaar the arms of the windmill whirred.

Mother led me to the lake,
swans glided past the palace;
by the sphinx-lions,
over the arched wooden bridge.
In the garden the angel rose in a Biblical vision;
her eyes looked upward,
vibrant wings spread on the air.

2

So I approach you again, angel
your wings tarnished yet graceful—
along this road Panzer divisions
rolled in to occupy the country,
and my Uncle Herman sneaked out
to gather firewood
under your watchful eye.

We walk by the pond
and cross the bridge over the sleeping swans.
Here my parents hid in the tall grass
spying on Opa and Oma strolling
and later they were married
in my childhood palace.

3

Angel, I recall you
on monuments, gravestones.
In mornings before school I saw you
on the Dutch war plaque,
when the light
broke through the curtains.

At twilight this park is a genesis
as we move through the shadows.
Night comes rustling
in the leaves,
and the fountain rises.

Opa

Five years old I stare up at him
mountainous in the white wicker chair,
puffing a Havana among the gardenias.
His hard blue eyes gaze through smoke
as his stained fingers reach for a deck of cards ...

He captained cargoes through risky waters,
watched ships flounder and people drown
in the *Zuider Zee*. He made a fortune:
Russian railways, German marks, South African mines—
lost it all in the Depression.

The Rhineland in the thirties,
drunken soldiers raised swastikas on jeeps.
Opa knew war was in the wind,
refused to deal with infiltrators.
The day Rotterdam was bombed
he cycled from Wassenaar to see his houses razed.

Always danger. In the darkened attic
he listened on headphones to BBC reports,
while below teenage daughters
listened to love songs in the occupied land.
In his eighties still
he skated the long canals with his sons.

Dinner is a late night ritual.
Opa stares at me for eating dessert quickly.
Later in the solarium he takes the deck
delicately in stiff, stained fingers,
lifts each king, queen and knight,
places them beside each other, making
the walls and the ceilings rise
into a blue and white house.

Work Camp

for Robert Veldhuisen

After the bombing of Rotterdam that was it.
Opa and you cycle through the flaming streets
past streaming refugees. There are new laws.
Jews vanish. An edict summons boys from villages.
When the commandant comes to the *Santhorslaan,*
you are on the soccer field.

On the station platform your family
is frozen in grief. You stick with friends.
Familiar water fades into alien country,
the Black Forest. Behind barbed wire
you sew uniforms long into the night.
Soccer on Sundays is the only freedom.
After months letters come less often.
Life is machines, uniforms, barbed wire sky.
A friend who tries to escape is shipped to Auschwitz.
At night planes drone overhead. You wait, listen.
One morning the compound is deserted
                                        and the gate is open ...

Elegy for Sarah

You were born under the pagan ring of Grianan
where the cold sun radiates
over the rough, spilling waters of Lough Swilly,
where the Earls exiled from Ulster sailed for Europe.
As a young woman you watched the stormy shore
in the cold air that blew down from the Skelp,
waiting for my grandfather
winding up from the crossing on his bicycle.

Three times I climbed the Celtic mount,
searched the hills for your place of birth,
was lost in the ridges and rumours of mountains,
the sudden streams.
From the summit I looked down
on the border were armoured vehicles moved.

Grandmother Sarah, as I search for you
along those Donegal border slopes,
through the rusty heather on Grianan flanks,
I think of you as a heroine in a Dickens' novel
or on the silver screen,
the white light falling through the clouds
across the mountain.

Woman in the Well

Adrian,
they said you were in prison
                              but you weren't.
Across the crackling fire you speak,
    "Allison, she's a big woman
          not many like her ...
    There, by the house, she was walk'n."
You raise a hand across flames—
    "I don't know how
          but she falls over a stone
down into the well
          an' we can hear her yell'n."

"We wander over an' calls down,"
'Are you ok?'
              "an' she starts a yell'n and holler'n
as if somethin's wrong with her
    splash'n down there like some big catfish woman
thrash'n about there
              like a whale."

'Why you good for nothing bastards,
can't you do anything to help a woman?'
An' we begin wander'n across the field
    an' gets a big hook
it bein' sharp as a harpoon."

"An' we says,
'Watch out, we're throw'n it down.'
All we hear's a splash, an' a yell.
    An' she's got the line
an' we're hugg'n an' heav'n
draw'n her up
              an' she's like some heavy fish
an we're pull'n it across the field.

And then
    there she is,
glisten'n like some fish woman,
  like you never seen
that woman angry
        com'n toward us."

A Child's History of Stamps

for Sean

I learned to handle the stamps as carefully
as the new born baby, cradling their edges.
More than any encyclopaedia
this was my gateway to the world.
Through telescopic windows I looked into
lush tropical countries: flowers, lions, butterflies,
Olympic runners caught in still motion.
    For the first time I saw Hitler—no Frankenstein—but
a man with a moustache, and the Spanish general whose
bald skull shone like a fierce moon, half-man, half-beast
and the Hungarian Revolution painted
on faded brown cloth, blood staining the print.
Whose tormented hands had it passed through?
I could hardly read its smudged lines,
peasants rising against the king's throne.
Each stamp was a different war scene—
death, suffering and victory.

Kaleidoscope

Christmas morning and I am seven.
I hold the kaleidoscope for the first time:
patterns change as exotic tapestries blossom.
Beyond the shores of waking I travel
past blue suns to orange planets,
gardens and menageries. I turn
the dream glass in my fingers
and things turn into one another:
silver dulcimers, red diamonds, sapphire waves.
I see myself in the old brick house:
relatives, presents and tangerines.
I see the illuminated fir, the winding road,
the little church, the river,
and the blue-gold earth, turning.

The Fathers

The Fathers of our streets were quiet
when they weren't working or drinking,
until they broke out in rage.
When David acted out the Howdy Doody puppet show
his father brooding like a dictator,
kicked us out into the cold spring air.
Kenny let us play in the loft of his barn:
we climbed up to a diving platform,
jumping and gliding into engulfing straw.
In the Victorian farmhouse his father shouted,
"How many times have I told you not to disturb the animals?"
as he spun Kenny across the floor.
Richard brought us over to look at his father's birds,
his basement was converted into an aviary.
Suddenly his father stomping down the stairs and shouting,
"What have I told you about having people over?"
Slapping his son, knocking his glasses from his face.
The Fathers were angry or silent.
Mr. Bishop, handsome like Ronald Colman,
suffered shell shock, never spoke of the war—
of the lash scars across his back
his fingers finding comfort only when planting
gladioli bulbs in the black earth.
The most unusual father was the German;
his house was full of secrets.
When the war was ending
he had limped miles
to surrender to the Allies.
Sometimes he looked at us with eyes
colder than the cobalt of a rifle barrel.
Other times his eyes were those of a wounded animal.

The Lost Glove

For my ninth birthday I got a red first-base glove—
not red, more maroon. Moulding the pocket to my hand,
I made fantastic catches in the Melody Road schoolyard.
Suddenly I couldn't find it anywhere.
I foraged rooms, trunks, the attic, wanting it to turn up.
There was rumour that Weber threw it into the pond
at the bottom of Habitant Drive and I dreamed
of rescuing it from the sludgy, turbid depths.

My baseball summer passed without a glove.
One day, Weber confesses defiantly.
I pushed him against the railing. I wanted to punch him,
but his mother pressed against the window pane was yelling,
"Leave him alone."
"He stole my glove."
He cowered in the cold wind.
I grabbed him by the neck and let him go …

This icy morning I think of that glove,
marooned deep in the earth—leather flower,
scarlet heart folded on its interlaced side
lost deep in layered glacial sand
becoming the colour of the earth, and the ink—
my own name now slowly dissolving into the earth.

Scoutmaster

He taught us the national anthem.
It was hard to hear his words;
his face was stitched with pink zippers.
He fought hand to hand with a German soldier
whom he killed, then caught shrapnel
from a bomb, struggled on
until he dropped onto rubble.

In winter, he took us on a long trek
through Boyd Conservation Park
for a war game, divided us into two groups,
which we named Allies and German.

For hours we
trekked, reading
the signs in the snow—
the broken twig
the lost Mars bar.
Down through brambles we moved
into imagined battle.

I don't know how long we climbed
the hills, wading waist high
through drifts of snow, looking
for the elusive enemy over
crests of snow, descending
dark brush, toward black water, pushing
aside wiry fences.

We never caught each other.
The cold was our biggest enemy:
the wind on the face, the freezing feet.
Finally, at the campfire
we were kid-soldiers leaning on trunks,
socks hanging on branches like dead birds.

He ordered us into lines
for the homeward trek,
breaking into his repertoire of army songs,
"Pack up your troubles in your old kit bag"
"Mademoiselle from Armentières, parlez-vous?"
as we were marching through the drifting snow.

Typing Class

Sitting down at my electric keyboard
I am Victor Borge of the piano
or Luis Borges alive in this storm of words.
Come let us compose the morning.
Suddenly I'm back in my grade nine typing class.
Miss Isabel Mendizabal, enchantress of
A Thousand and One High School Nights,
held my fingers arched high above
unknown keys and suggested,
"You have fine fingers for the piano,"
then gave me the lowest
                    typing mark in the history of Emery.
A mad secretarial conductor, she held the cane,
decoded the alphabet in coloured combinations
of the chemical table of elements
in the classroom where
thirty-three future secretaries
punched out keys with the precision of medical formulae:
"ASDF and now HJKL and WERT and UIOP"
using Doctor Seuss combinations.
"Dog sat on the cat."
"Man ran on the moon."
The bells in the room gone wild like a music
of Mussorgsky's *Night on Bald Mountain*.

Milkweed

A thirteen-year old boy in the ravine
lifts the milkweed pod through mauve sky upward,
releases seeds to the moon.
          The weed, not flower, not jack-in-the-pulpit,
but rough skin, nodules,
   bumps, hard metacarpal,
        faded puce, mole fur, velvet-ridged, a broken boat.
Once in public school we drew the pod
until it became a thousand things:
a clown striped banana,
a green beaked parrot perched in the wind
or a mouth opening revealing
soft down skin
      with tiny seeds that resembled
delicate Japanese prints.
The pod breaks open, launches its seeds,
humming-bird's tail,
like decorations of an Irish Christmas tree.
When blowing in the wind
they dance, circles rise, spin and drop jazzy rhythms
words … rising … rushing …
      domestic sputniks
playful gyroscopes
    drifting stars.
At thirteen, I flip open its coarse green-tufted skin
among tall frosted grass
   they float up a ladder of lace,
  space pods
       spiralling through the mist
        toward the moon—
      their own milky way.

Relics

"Propriété Privée, défense de passer"
We push open the saloon doors
into the cabin, great stone walls intact,
pans, like helmets, rot in the dust.

In woods bottles stick through ice—
clear decanters, pink Revlon glass, Gattuso jars.
Search the rust and jewelled fragments ...
    You are eight, push sand aside to find an Egyptian vase,
hieroglyphs of wild birds, slaves, and pharaohs.
    You are ten, check the wavering tents,
Wasaga Beach, the lost doubloons in the sand.

Pry emerald loose, bone from icy shoal.
Push apart limbs among dazzling ice ...
Broken bottles sink into the earth;
moss tongues curl around smooth bellies.
There are no maple syrup cans, only Javex glass.
Somewhere, huzza of hydroplane or buzz saw—
there in the bushes a crushed fuselage
corroded cone and shredded tire,
a crumpled Cessna—
                the last maple syrup tank.
Vines coil around it,
the hydra dragging it slowly underground.

Cold shadows grow over
giant blocks of a Gothic barn
where horses, unharnessed for the night
breathed fiery breath into violet air.
A broken stagecoach rim,
a lost sundial, leans against a trunk.

Kneeling, I find
the great rusted femurs
   the sand-papered ribs
thick bolted teeth
fine line of the jaw—
     the maple sled just as it stopped running,
the bright invisible growth everywhere.

Burnt Island Lake

1

Nowhere to land. All campsites filled.
I hold the fatigued paddle.
Through open water we race against declining light.
Ahead is barren shore: twisted roots,
blasted trees, forbidden place.

2

Dark hills gather crimson blood-light.
I jump into cool violet water,
swim over fish-shaped rocks among trunks,
beak of branch speaks water tongue.
Roots swirl out of stone legends:
Laocoön and his sons strangled by serpents,
bison sockets glare out of waves.

In night's blue geometry
stars pulse beyond Algonquin hills.
Things speak: the forest waves
to the rhythm of wind and water.
I sit on the rim of the rocks,
watch firelight dance over waves,
watch fire flow up through the rock bowl
as anger rises from dark caves.
The lonely raven's cry
and the raw laughter of loons
ring through lost mythologies
of Burnt Island Lake.

3

All night I listen
to the cardiac rhythm of the waves,
to the bears crawling,
raccoons scavenging, forest walking.

A nomad I came to these broken shores,
shattered roots. Trees cry,
it is in your ruins you find pain;
make your words sing
among twisted branches and cold currents
forging your life, bringing you closer
                    to the voices of the earth.

Spoon

To practice poems
hold the spoon,
feel the weight of the metal
on your fingertips,
the way the bubble
shows the carpenter
the level of the line.
To practice poems
try to ignore the noises of children
(you cannot ignore the children's noises),
but hold the spoon
(your son is also looking for a spoon).
Look at its lines,
how well they are shaped
to its tapered form,
the long neck opening out into the elliptical head.
Observe how the lines
circle the metal like natural striations
formed not of the earth
but of the movement of the mouth
and the fingers upon it.
Observe the peculiar colour
of rust and silver.
Ignore the crests and words
(although you cannot fail to see
this is an Irish hotel with a Royal Crown crest
on opposite sides).
To practice poems
you must hold the spoon
more consciously than you would a pen,
feel its form and its smooth function.
Observe, too, how the form is not of the earth
but transformed from the metal out of the earth
deep fires, millions of years before.

If you want to practice poems,
put the spoon into your mouth.
Feel your lips around it,
sounds, shapes, textures, flavours.
Feel how it nourishes you
with its meats, vegetables, and fruit,
how it takes them from the earth into you.

Night Vision

Walking out to the log cabin for firewood,
I gaze toward the great curved screen of sky
to see the Big Dipper,
                              then cast my eyes further afield
to the Little Dipper
and the warrior with his studded buckle.
There on the horizon behind the silo
I see an orange volcanic bubble
of the slow rising moon
                              (sixty-eight miles per second)
throwing its light over the cold snowscape
just beyond the tower and the branches of the trees.
And I run across the snow to bring
you shivering in a dressing gown
to look upon this wildly improbable moon.

Ultrasound

for Emma

Sitting in the waiting room
I scan the paintings, thinking of child
at the shifting perspectives of Escher,
Chagall's horses and chickens
swirling through a turbulence of colour.

Focusing on the screen I try to get
a perspective on it. The doctor divines the foetal form;
you make your appearance on black and white TV,
floating between the pelvic fissures of the earth.

Alien space explorers, we probe dark depths
where, star child, you glimmer
within the grey possibilities of Mother.
Your heart pumps luminously in underwater breathing.
Amphibian, you are paddling through the underworld.
I see you for the first time, phantom child.

And the day you were born
the most radiant yellow bird
sang from our plum tree.

Hippocrates in the Pharmacy

A blue transparent cranium,
bust of modern man
absorbs light from medical paraphernalia.
Smooth plastic features offer
an illusion of peering into the mind,
yet reflect only more blue,
tropical Laurentian ink
or Caribbean poster seas.

The transparency of blue
as thought itself
shines in Arctic clarity,
revealing nothing,
                              the nothing that is.

Hippocrates swore allegiance to Apollo,
not this android stare
which sees man denuded of himself.
Surrounded by medicine for every ailment
I remember the Greek busts
when stone became skin, and wisdom
spoke through craggy cheeks and rough-hewn brows.

Circle the modern mind
that attracts itself by a reflection of itself.
The poster boys in dark glasses
smiling with the blindness of style.

The Glass Blower

Beyond his shoulder horses run:
he breathes flame into glass,
moulds the air into clear forms,
original as the first time I saw television
where a sculptor modeled the animals of Genesis.

Poised in the centre of the spellbound crowd
he casts his material in a sleight of hand,
his eyes are charged with cosmic gaiety
as he exhales glass into musical form:
fine tubes, soft angles and treble clefs.

An animal tamer, he draws shapes
out of the wilderness into the barely animal.
In the glass-roofed coliseum,
beyond the hushed crowd
the equestrians ride roughly over the hard earth.

With light flourishing gestures
he inspires perfect rhythms
as his lips blow glass into forms,
precise as a French horn player's notes.

These are no blue souvenir lions,
no frozen tiger-angelfish,
but light, form and energy;
his eyes flash as he breathes fire into glass.
the horses in the coliseum running.

The Shape of the Earth

Here the earth curves before our eyes,
rolls away, down toward clear horizons.

And it strikes your eye as a page
as you write upon it now in new forms.

The plants and trees become words,
the hills and ponds, the heart and eyes.

The land is new in this light
where the city no longer holds,

as you stand alone before the horizon and
the light sounds above the earth

in the clarity of a chime. And you write upon
the wide earth, under the silver span of

sky, over the rolling land where now
you feel the rim of the circle

and the power of the line.

Blackout

Outside, the city is captured in a freeze frame. The moment is held in the silence of the silver screen. Orange leaves are suspended in crystal; the boughs are black in silicon transparency, and the streets glazed in treachery. The world is beautiful and dangerous as branches break the circuits and ice pellets nick cars and passengers.

At night the city is given over to darkness. I walk out through the blackened streets lit only by yellow flares. The houses are lonely and fragile, crouched in larger shadows. People venture out of need, to clear a path, to buy candles and try to get out of where they are. Blackout. Notions. Shapes. Tyrannosaurian plough.

In darkness, we become primitive men wandering around caves in fear, searching for fire. More likely, it's the actual fear that one has had in Belfast, Beirut, or anywhere—close to what we could be. Here and there boys with sticks swipe at ice-knives, nomads roaming in darkness ...

Mountain Walk

Behind me the lovers sit in their relic cars as I stand above
the shoal, listen to the surf break over subterranean life. On this
primordial shore the land slowly rises from the dolphin-blue and
amphibians crawl through the snowy tide. Wind sweeps through
tentacles of this coral sea among intimate lost voices.

Through the blurred pines I climb toward the peak of lights—the
four moons of Jupiter. Rain pellets crack the snow in unknown codes.
I look for signs, try to humanize this landscape with words, but there
is only the wind speaking in dumb tones. The black branches are
twisted girders, melted iron, torn cables. And the trees. What are
they? Wounded soldiers speaking of their deaths, shamans chanting
their prophecies.

The path leads to a lifeless arena, an empty proscenium. No stairs,
a flagless pole, outspread tablets I cannot decipher, a row of empty
tripods. Eerie light hovers over frozen cairns, hulks. Down in the mist
an aqueous eye stares at me. The wind whines through the red earth.

Snow

Are there not treasures in the snow? It awakens me to colour
and forms out of its anonymity. Beneath its smooth surface I see
idiosyncrasies: microprisms breaking into chromatic scales ...
myriad globes glowing ... glacial spores blossoming ...

What I love is the mathematical precision with which it covers the
earth in frozen solutions. As I walk across the *tabula rasa*, deeper into
the shifting planes, there is a geometric excitement: fine logarithms,
musical phrases, a wonderful amnesia. Snowflakes, words tumble—
changing infinities in fin-like speed. New possibilities whirl out of
violet haloes and the Milky Way.

Snow paradise. Carousels of evening horns and bells. You cover
everything in a philosophical eloquence.

Rain

There are days like today when all I want is rain. Rain, the rich paradox, has a misty clarity continually transforming light and shape. Rain makes me feel the presence of that light.

In this darkening twilight, riding the shuttle bus, I am in love with all the rainy days, ambiguous and naked like forgotten lovers. Words breathe upon the windowpane. I can just make out the chaotic traffic ... the work camps ... the space way ... the Christmas tree ... Picasso's and the erotic floor show in the heavens ... and there in the clouds floats an orange bar, a de Kooning ...

In the moist suspension I spin on through the rain, the swimmer as he breaks the waves. In tangible silence I glide through the twilight trajectory, toward the dark comfortable place I call home.

Midnight

My favourite hour. How comfortable to sit here listening to the refrigerator humming, the syncopation of the clock, the midnight bus braking: the warming up of an orchestra.

After a long day's journey I reach the shore and look out on sleep's dark breakers. Today we painted a wall, not much mind you—but those old green flowers are finally gone. We can hang pictures *there*. But to get back to midnight, not the beach, but the wide red table that spreads before me like a mesa. In the landscape are walnuts, green grapes, Spiderman, and wooden Russian dolls. My thought stops. I step outside myself. I am the stranger walking by the sea.

Midnight, my favourite hour, when the refrigerator is an Arctic piano. After the hockey game last night, I drove out into the unrecognizable mauve city. On the mountain's edge the boy and girl drank, danced, and sang into the wind.

On the edge be near the power, not the guardian of thought. Be the stranger, the reader. Come, the scherzo is over. Already the drum of the clock is fading and the piano plays softly like a cardiogram. Listen, the late night bus revellers, the voices of sleep. The clock steps draw you closer to the waves. Fatigue, like a friend, takes you into the weird night, childhood. Now after travelling all day, relearn the world. Stranger, the sea is here. Forget and welcome.

Emery
(1998)

Two Maps of Emery

Open the book and find the map of Emery,
find the village which no longer exists,
the lots of the original settlers.
Trace the pattern of their settlement,
their lots and their concessions:
the Devins came with Governor Simcoe,
Crossons trekked by horse from Pennsylvania,
Rowntrees and Watsons emigrated from England,
Duncans and Griffiths from Ireland.

Examine the modern map of Emery
circa 1948, the year of my birth.
Look at the lines on the map,
how they lead beyond the page
into the fields and orchards I knew,
to barbed wire fences that I climbed.

Turn the pages to discover the history of the village.
Look at the buildings on the map
drawn by Marion Rowntree in the 1940s:
the blacksmith shop, the carriage shop,
the shingle mill, the community hall.
Look for the general store, the stable,
the post office and the railway station.
Find the Methodist church and Emery Public School.

Who are these farmers that ploughed the fields,
their tractors navigating the warm sea of wheat?
Who are the soldiers whose names are
engraved on the monument?
What stories are hidden under the fading lines of this stone?
Whose faces are in the photo of Emery Public School?
Who lived in the abandoned houses that I explored?

During the late fifties our lives intersected briefly.
I watched farmers leaning on fences,
neighbours talking about their work.
Slowly new roads and houses rose on subdivision grids;
the farmers' fences broke and fields faded,
the end of a silent film.

For years I've been away,
yet their houses have haunted my dreams.
The farmers' voices said, "Turn from your work.
Return to a place that is no longer there."
I dream of a clear river that flows through Emery,
of a tree that grows through school windows.
"Journey," say the voices, "to find your history.
Here is the place you are looking for."

The Farmhouse

That first fall we climbed toward the farmhouse
at the top of Emery hill. Near the ravine ridge
we entered the wooden hut and
looked down into the well,
wondering where the water came from.

When my friend, Les and I looked up at the house,
the farmer and his dog were bearing down on us;
we turned and ran down the hill through the marsh,
with the dog chasing us, and the farmer waving his shotgun,
shouting, "Stay off my land."

Months later, still afraid of that man,
we walked again toward the then deserted farmhouse.
Over rusty mattresses we crawled,
sneaked past the wrecked Studebaker.
We opened the door
child anthropologists entering an ancient tomb.

Inside, the house was intact:
coal oil lamps, mirrors, a wash stand, doilies,
a church calendar, "God Bless Our Home."
It was as though they had just moved out.

We opened a small black trunk, a treasure chest
and found copies of *The Globe and Mail*
going back to the beginning of the war
and in the wind I hear
Walter Cronkite's deep voice speaking of the Battle of Arnhem.

Turning the yellowed pages,
I thought of the old man overseas
as I read headlines—Stalingrad, Normandy, El Alamein,
and studied photos of Churchill and Roosevelt,
resembling old trading cards.

The next week, in the cold November chill,
I saw this black trunk in the Gulfstream schoolyard,
the broken chest spilling out its papers
like calendar pages in an old movie
clinging to the wire of the Frost fence.

A few months before, families were still out
doing the wash, pumping water, feeding animals—
and then they were gone.
Only the mouldy smell of mattresses,
rust stained refrigerators
and the ruined walls of the farmhouse remained,
and the memory of that nameless farmer
like an old god guarding the hilltop.

The Pump

As I was listening to the farmer Charlie Grubbe talk
about the old Emery schoolhouse pump,
slowly in pieces the memories come back.

Now in the hot late August afternoon,
when I'm picking pears from the farmer's orchard
and putting them into a wicker basket,
                    I see the rusty pump
with its broken wooden base.

Pumping it up and down,
I hear a groan,
a drawing sound
from somewhere deep in the earth,
then, the sound of rising water
gushing out in spurts.

I cup water in my palms,
to taste it,
splash it on my face,
open my eyes through dust
to see again:
the school, the football field
with the sagging uprights,
the grey gravestones leaning
beyond the waving wheat.
Here I'm standing in the full sunshine,
at the crossroads of Emery.

The Abandoned Church of Emery

The church was empty,
no pews or Bibles.
Inside the smooth concrete floor
was cool as a hockey arena in summertime.
Broken stained glass panes,
ruby and amethyst,
were lying on the floor
along with rectangles of hopscotch
with swear words drawn by children
and big valentine hearts
with initials I tried to decode.
The pulpit was solitary.
In cold darkness
I hear the ghost of the minister,
the choir singing hymns
as wind rustles
through chestnut trees,
broken panes of framed sky.

Chestnuts

We headed north in quest of chestnuts,
the last adventure of the summer before school began.
With sticks we knocked them down,
split green leather rind to find grey-white nuts.
Later, we would harden them in the oven,
drill the hole, carefully thread with shoelaces
and take them into the schoolyard
for the conker battles.

Now, poring over blank maps and concession lines,
the trees shine again on red brick houses in green fields.
At the end of our scavenger hunt
that encompassed the territory of dying farms,
I remember the tree on the Duncan farmhouse with
window curtains blowing into the form of a girl,
the tree on Main Street where the Kilmers
played among the ruined farm machinery,
and the one by the Riley's white house
shimmering filaments in late August heat.

The most productive tree of all
stood between the Emery schoolhouse and the church
where we found chestnuts in the grass,
carried them to the stone war monument
to break the sharp shells open,
the spikes piercing the skin on our hands.
Then we headed home
with chestnuts ripening in our pockets.

Grandmothers

We would see the grandparents of friends
from Italy or Germany draped in black:
handkerchiefs, shawls, dresses, stockings, shoes.
Their bronzed faces were wrinkled, with moles and facial hair,
witches from Grimm's fairy tales.
We would see them at Italian Gardens,
trying to hold on to their granddaughters
who danced in the wind just out of their reach.
They looked at us as if we were strangers of the new world.
They would arrive in summer,
sit on porches and speak in foreign tongues.
Sometimes they would sniffle or wave,
but dismiss us with an uncomprehending gaze
when we would ride by on our bikes
and nod imperceptibly toward them.
If we got close enough, they lightly smiled,
so lightly, as they dabbed their handkerchiefs to their eyes,
calling out to offspring who no longer understood them.
Oma, dressed in a neat grey suit from Holland,
had become distant and silent with the years,
talked mostly with her eyes, her smile,
her hands reaching awkwardly towards me ...

The Toys of Johnny Wolf

He got off the school bus
holding his crutches in one hand,
stepped awkwardly down.
His shy eyes turned away
as he limped before us
across Tumpane schoolyard.

"He broke his leg trying to fly,"
Karl, his brother, said slyly.

Later that fall he brought
a hand grenade to "Show and Tell."
"Evacuate the room," ordered the kindergarten teacher
while children ran screaming down the hall.
Dumbfounded, he stood in the doorway,
wondering why everyone had deserted him.

He led me down
into the unfinished rec room
behind the rumbling furnace
to show me his father's collection.
I held the bronze bullets
and the hand grenade
like a small green pineapple,
a Mattel toy, only heavier.

Black Creek Pioneer Village

I linger under the loft in the alcove of the barn,
look through the panes of the frosted window
and for a moment here
I imagine a Christmas in 1840 in York.
Outside the wind blowing.
I could see a girl in the room of the house
with ruffled petticoats holding her porcelain doll,
a boy in Victorian clothes kneeling over his steel toy train.
"Time to move on, students," says Mr. Smallbridge.
We climb onto the horse-drawn hay wagon,
which lumbers across the dusty road of Steeles.

In Joseph Stong's big barn
I touch barley rakes, pitchforks,
feel gritty wooden surfaces of butter churns.
As I stand in the wide doorway,
a cold wind blowing around us,
and the old man talks about threshing,
"This was the way we separated wheat from chaff."
I lift up the fallen wheat,
letting it trickle in streams of golden grain;
the dusty chaff blows away, a parable of Judgment Day.

I am walking here,
trying to place myself a hundred years ago,
still feeling the grain in my palm.
In the late autumn
at twilight I clamber up the hillside,
pause before a garden,
leaning on the fence
I inhale rich scents slowly, pronounce under my breath:
tarragon, thyme, sage, coriander ...

Icebreakers

Spring draws us out of school
    through the subdivision
        out across fields to the hill.
          We slide down the mud runway
             into the plaster of Paris ravine
               where the stream bursts its ridged banks.
          We jump over swells and ice-clefts
        mounds of dog-brown snow as
      water charges through the pipe grate;
    we are on the ice one last time this year
and the world is flowing again.
    My eye follows the sweeping water—
        there an otter dives and is gone—
      down to the oxbow and side spit
        to where water widens at the gap
          flowing beyond forests of the peninsula.
         I hear the sound of woodwinds
        through the tinkling ice
        as currents carry suburban garbage.
      Beyond the leaning reeds
    we crawl onto the thin edge,
find crevices and ice bridges,
        snap down the overhangs
         and we become icebreakers
            lumberjacks balancing on rolling logs,
    rock'n'rollin' on the slippery edges
    singing in the spring water
  until the ice cracks
and we slide down into the drink
    where water rises to our red rims and over,
      sink down into the ultimate soaker.
        (Still, when no one is looking
          you can go back to being an icebreaker).

Playing Hockey on Crang's Pond

for Dale Ritch

We dreamed of playing at the Maple Leaf Gardens,
waited for *Hockey Night in Canada* following
The Plouffe Family, Don Messer's Jubilee,
and the chorus of the Esso commercial
What a great, great feeling,
what a wonderful sense
of pure enjoyment and of confidence ...

At the end of the fifties
the place to play hockey was at Crang's Pond.
We played with the Wolf brothers, Upton and Ritch,
tightening skates on the frozen banks
striding onto the ice, clearing the rink and choosing sides.

Each game was different:
the swerves, the dekes, glides, passing and shooting—
to break through the defense
bearing down on the goalie
(the way I saw Béliveau or Mahovlich move),
aiming for a corner by the boot post into the snow net.
After the breathy exhaustion of the sudden death goal,
we left our indecipherable signatures on the dark ice.

We always tried to prolong the hockey season
despite the water lapping the reedy pond's edge
and the ice split not far from us,
getting softer, turning a little gold.
Taking off our coats and gloves
we played the game into the warm afternoon until
the whole damned pond sagged and cracked beneath us.

Italian Gardens

Those summer weekends thousands of Italians
and the local kids converged on the old Rowntree farm.
Across from the house there was a dance floor,
a bandshell with a jukebox, and behind it,
and a dressing room for the swimming pool.

The crowded terrazzo floor spun with couples.
Italian men with their new Canadian girlfriends
swirled into this rock'n'roll fever.
Sausages on grills spluttered under bannered tents;
bachelors ate thick crusted pizza
drank bottled Brio and licked Spumoni.
Accordions squeezed out "Volare."
There were flags, greased pole climbers, diving clowns,
champion European cyclists in spandex circling the track,
lines of whiskered Italian grandmothers
dressed in black, staring at the dancers,
holding their granddaughters
with their puffy, out of place crinolines in check.

There were extraordinary days: Gina Lollobrigida sashayed
through the bee-humming apple orchards like the Queen of Sheba.
Bobby Curtola rock'n'rolled in the bandshell.
NHL All-stars Lou Fontinato, Carl Brewer, Frank Mahovlich
                              played baseball on the diamond.

Always the music emanated from the bandshell
decorated with panthers and tigers in pastel jungles.
Inside change rooms boys looked
through the knotholes at the women undressing
(warned by younger girls
who stuck pins through the holes)
as they sought a vision of breast or fiery bush.

There were young couples who sauntered
into the woods as men with binoculars
peered like spies in war movies.
On Sunday mornings the priest celebrated Mass,
intoned Latin over the terrazzo dance floor,
atoned for the sins of the day before.

French Dictation

Seeing the poster in the college hallway,
Dictée des Amériques 1994
I remember the piercing words
coming from the green plastic tape recorder,
Écoutez, *n'écrivez pas!*—
the shrill voice of a dictator from the Franco-Prussian War.
It was a voice calculated to evoke fear,
Et les poules de Monsieur Dupuis ... VIRGULE,
sounds of panic, swirling turbulence,
a needle punctures the skin.
I spin like Lloyd Bridges in *Sea Hunt*
bubbles bursting around my twisted mask
drifting to the bottom of the sea—
et puis, les poules dans le jardin
deviennent ivres ... POINT D'EXCLAMATION!
The words came fast like a fusillade.
The verbs lined up like battalions on a battlefield:
passé composé, futur antérieur, futur conditionnel ...
The dictator droned on about the drunken chickens
and my pen limped across the page,
anticipating the impending red casualties ...

Hitchhiking from Algeciras to Madrid,
an eccentric Moroccan threatened
to throw me into the night of the Spanish desert.
The only way to remain in the car was to speak French:
every noun, every verb, every phrase I could remember,
the works of French 101: *L'étranger, Huis clos*
Le Livre de mon ami—
making up the language as I went along,
hearing the sound of the dictator's voice,
"*Ecoutez, n'écrivez pas.*"
Mesa forms in the desert became wolves
Shadows of trees became bandits.

Then the language became my ally,
allowing me to stay in the safety of the car
mile after mile after mile.
And so I talked about *mauvaise foi,*
Meursault, *un autre Arabe*
Rimbaud, *le dérangement de tous les sens*
Baudelaire, *la nature est un temple.*
I told the driver it didn't matter if the car
wasn't safe, and the insurance had run out.
Then I remembered the rules,
felt the rhythm of the phrases.
I talked of the virtues of Morocco:
les grands lacs, les montagnes, la mer.
I talked about anything *sous le soleil*
just to stay in the car
just to get to Madrid ...
parle de de Gaulle, parle de Québec
parle de Garde civile et parle de Franco
parle de Lorca
parle de l'amour
parle de fromage
parle de vin, de fleurs,
de Paris, de Londres
parle de la neige du Canada
mais ne parle pas en anglais.
We drove past the great fallen castles,
spoke of the words of the dictator.
Then *les mots sont mes amis.*
The car, a strange wide-finned ambulance
rumbled through the wild sea-blue Spanish night.

The Journey of Isaac Devins

Here I am an eighty-year-old man, thinking.
For the last time I survey the cabin,
the fields and hills of Emery,
the Humber Valley where I spent my life.
My wife Polly calls out,
"Isaac, you were never good at farewells."

We were here from the beginning.
I remember the years of war with America.
For weeks my father, Abraham, would be gone fighting.
Mother and us children crammed into the smoky cabin.
We had no friends. Who were your friends?

The war dragged on and we began the long journey north.
We saw the British soldiers dead in the fields,
the lines of wounded prisoners.
With Governor Simcoe we crossed Ontario Lake
to safer British territory. When the fog cleared
we lifted our eyes to the unsettled shores:
this was to be our land.

So much to be done in those early months
clearing the land at the mouth of the Don,
hacking out the bush for the Yonge Highway.
Elizabeth, our first child, was born in the Governor's tent.
Lady Simcoe said, "She is the first child born in the colony."

Nicholas and me built the King's Mill for the Governor.
We worked hard, hauling stone from the Humber River,
felling high timber from the smoky forests,
our horses grunting in the mud.
Aboriginals did not attack us,
only broke fences, stole wood.

The King's Mill rose like a tower,
the river turning the wheel into energy,
the grain into bread and whiskey.

I said goodbye to my father and brothers.
Passing by the King's Highway, through Weston
we pushed our barge against late spring currents,
and when it shallowed, Elizabeth and Hannah jumped in.
Osprey and eagles swooped overhead,
the spawning salmon swished around us,
deer paused.

Rounding the bend I see my land,
the river, the tall stands of pine,
the sandbanks, hills that rolled.
Near the Oxbow I built my cabin.
My son James shared a plug of tobacco
with an Aboriginal chief;
he laughed at my jokes.
The river flows through the valley
past the ruins of the King's Mill.
I was miller, builder, surveyor, lumberman.
My sons and daughters will farm this land
for generations, as I have farmed, I hope.
Polly is waving to me—
it is time to leave.

Robert Grubb

They have renamed St. Andrews, calling it Thistletown—
it sounds more like a weed than a town.
If Father were alive today, he would be angry.
His legacy is beginning to fade.
I received one hundred pounds from his estate,
my brother "Brae Burn."
That was not fortunate either.
Last year when it burned down,
Whitrock and Eliza, my sister,
were lucky to escape with their lives.
The maid ran outside half "nakit,"
—as Robert Burns would say—into the full daylight.
Far from Edinburgh or New York we must live.
On the edge of my father's account books,
outside the realm of his figures
I write about the love of dancing and a woman.

While Father was alive,
there were never parties at the house on New Year's Eve,
but this last night the tables were set with
pâtisseries, hors d'oeuvres—delicacies of all sorts
and we danced until three in the morning.

Father's portrait still dominates the room.
Albion Road is falling into disrepair.
Grand Trunk is building a railway through Weston
and my father's company in due course will be bankrupt.
I am Robert, his eccentric son.
I write my poems on the margins of his life.

Clairvoyant

for Patty

There are some who say I'm a witch,
avoid me as if I'm possessed,
afraid I'll determine something in their future.
When I'm silently rocking, speaking to myself,
I see things in the lightning in the night clouds.
Last year I dreamed of rustlers and convinced the men
that we must stay up and we caught them thieves like I said we would.

Don't ask me how it works,
how the moonlight falls just right in the field
where the rabbit sits vigilant in the grass,
the peculiar hush of wind on water announcing a storm.
I know it as I know the weave of my knitting.
I could see that the Devins' girl would drown in the pond.

They say I have healing hands
have power to let pain go.
I could tell them if they would listen.
I know that the heart hears its own blood beating,
as will has its own special warmth that can save you,
the pain leaves—you cannot fight the current.

I've sat up nights and felt myself whole as a landscape.
I think that there are dangers in the dark.
Even my husband, especially he, should believe in this power,
but he is a man of few words who trusts his work
and what he can make with his hands.

My power comes from my secret knowing.
There are many things that men have to learn,
but they go on earning their living;
my living is already learned right here
rocking in my night chair,
seeing the dark side of the moon.

The Day Orrie Trueman Climbed
the Emery Schoolhouse Tower

Charlie Grubbe and Aubrey Ella recall certain days:
the day teacher Macdonald shook Castator
until the nails came out of his desk,
the day that Walter Lund dropped dead in a baseball game,
and the day Orrie Trueman climbed the school bell tower.
Dared by the boys to ring the bell
he began to climb the bricks on the south side,
finding a foothold in the half-inch edges
and using them like rungs on a ladder, he climbed up into the sky.
As he climbed he could see
Art Peeler's dumbfounded face at the window.
He could see his classmates getting smaller.
His climb would be something special:
something the boys would talk about,
maybe even the girls would notice,
something to give him a place in the school.

When Orrie finally stood on the rooftop of Emery
and rang the clapper, the village stopped.
Probably, his mother ran out of the kitchen door,
her tea towel wrapped around her wet hands.
His stepfather walked out of the barn and took off his hat.
Jennie Gillis stopped scattering grain to the chickens.
Below him the pupils shouted and whistled.
He heard the sound of the strap in the principal's voice.
It didn't matter as long as he stood at the summit.
It made him forget about losing at soccer.
It made him forget about wearing the dunce cap.
Years later, when reveille awoke Orrie
and the sun glared down over the battlefield of the Sahara,
he stood again in the school tower and rang the bell over Emery.

Gladys Graham at Ravensbrück:
an Imaginary Letter to Elizabeth Arden

Dear Sister,
> You would not recognize me I have grown so gaunt:
my eyes hollowed, my lips cracked.
When my fingers grasp the barbed wire fence
I look to freedom beyond ...
I watch the women walking aimlessly,
imprisoned for their resistance. I miss my life
mon mari, Paris, la langue française—
on fait des conjugaisons
je serai, tu seras, il sera
il n'y a pas d'autres choses à faire
ah, j'oublie, Florence
tu n'as jamais pu apprendre le français.
Ravensbrück is a horrible place:
guards with guns and hard faces.
Before the war in Paris at a dinner party
you called Herr Göring a fat pig.
How far you have come since the days
when we walked along the path from the log cabin in Emery
and you said, "I will be the richest little woman in the world."
Mais, c'était charmant, le petit Emery,
avec ses champs, ses collines et la Rivière Humber
et notre père *qui parlait toujours de chevaux de race.*
I had no choice. We could not let the allied pilots
be taken, had to get them back to England.
Sometimes, I think I'll go mad,
but you keep me sane, Florence.
There will be an end to this,
"Drink lots of water, flush out the poisons," you said.
So we have, and we will survive.
This letter will not leave my mind,
but know that I am well.
Someday, you will see I am alive.

Searching for the Log Cabin of Elizabeth Arden

What am I doing here at the edge of the city,
in the smoky heart of North York's industrial wasteland,
running across the highway ramp, and climbing
over this nine foot fence into a no trespassing zone?
Jack Devins said the "cosmetic queen" grew up in a log cabin
just off the seventh and Jean Dalziel had pointed to this wood.

And here I am in this reedy swamp, pushing through
apple trees grown as thick as thorned limbs,
looking for any relic that might lead to her cabin.
The November night is already closing in.
She was born New Year's Eve, 1879
on the Pine Ridge Road in the White Pigeon Hotel
and christened Florence Nightingale Graham.

Before me a pile of ruins, shattered concrete steps,
an RCA television set, a smashed Canada Dry tin,
a plastic chemical container with a lethal X.
I move on through pine trees to a broken cistern,
and reaching down I lift a concrete block
and inhale the scent of mint.

Here is the laneway where her father,
the huckster with his horse and wagon,
would have trudged home with his wares.
I feel the fence with its splintered boards
bony as his stubborn Scottish fingers
and I imagine the old log cabin standing here.
She would have looked out upon this marsh
dreaming already of becoming Elizabeth Arden,
taking the name from Lord Tennyson's poem.
In her Fifth Avenue salon she would remember this forest,
gazing at her Chagalls with their crazy steeples and flying cows,
recall riding to Emery with her father on horseback,

seeing the ghostly Lawder giants returning from the mill,
hearing the teasing of the Castator boys,
smelling the horse manure from the Devins' stable,
skipping with Mary Hopcroft as the bell rang in the schoolyard.

She took her own name, Graham, for her stables.
Her horse, "Jet Pilot," prevailed, and she stood
in the winner's circle at Churchill Downs,
thinking of her father who raced thoroughbreds in Cornwall
to win his young bride over
before eloping to the end of the world.

Sometimes she would return to her Emery friends,
arrive at their farmhouses in a chauffeur-driven limousine.
At the opening of Black Creek Pioneer Village, her last visit,
her father's landlord, Mr. Dalziel, welcomed Florence.
"She is now Elizabeth Arden," whispered her secretary,
"It's the first time I've seen Miss Arden cry."

Charlie Grubbe's Tour of Grouse Hill

Through the whispering grass we move.
        Charlie stops ...
                "Ah, what's this?"
Clearing the grass with his feet he finds a dip in the earth.
        "Around here about twenty feet from the river
my father dug a well.
The hired hand, an Englishman, spent all one winter
digging a trench up the hill.
        In the spring, the river
flooded the well and filled it up with silt.
We never found good water."

After Charlie Grubbe left, these ravines became mine.
I poled with the giant red haired boy across the pond.
I wandered like a vagabond among autumn hills.
I collected the oak leaves to press in Loblaw's book of knowledge.
I blew milkweed pods toward the mist-blown moon.
I was Dr. Leakey searching for Olduvai man.
I was Robinson Crusoe stranded on Rabbit Island.
I was Superman flying from the high embankment.
I was Turok, Son of Stone finding blind fish in sewer pipe caves.
I whirred through eons in H.G. Wells' The Time Machine.

We move toward the mouth of Emery Creek.
        Across the river is the Grubbe homestead, "Brae Burn."
"There is an oxbow
                around here somewhere;
there were three on the deed.
                  The mouth of the creek
should be just beyond
                the hill and tower.

There, push this away ...
                    here we are.
                                   The Humber still has a good flow.
And there,"
          he points to the ridge,
                                  "is the old road that led to the barn."

At the corner of Coronado Court Charlie stops the truck;
he recognizes a pine tree that stood at the gateway,
two hundred feet from his house ...
This is familiar territory. Gulfstream Public School
I trace my Globe and Mail *route,*
recalling the names ... St. Lucie, Tampa Terrace
Azalea Court, Coral Gable, and Gulfstream.
What mad developer had dreamed up these names?

This was Grouse Hill where the first school was built in 1834.
The barn was out there by Azalea Court.
This is where the Griffith brothers built the Orange Lodge in 1845,
then it was turned into an icehouse.
A larger Home Circle Community Hall was built
then reassembled up at Emery.
And finally at the end of the fifties
Kenny Foster's father used the boards for a chicken coop in Milton.

The barn is here, where, on a December morning in 1942,
George Grubbe (in the photograph a man holding a kitten
in front of the poor well and the icehouse)
was walking the bull in the barnyard
when something happened—either he had a heart attack or
slipped on a piece of black ice—and when he fell the bull
stepped on his neck. Charlie heard him cry out,
carried him to the car and drove him to Humber Memorial
where, on the operating table two hours later, he died.

It's the old red house like a phantom ship I remember
moored in the fog like one of Opa's old sailing vessels.
Before its facade I played my first game of pond hockey;
the blank half-deserted windows stared
as silent spectators from a lost legacy
while the Wallace brothers, the big Swede and I
chased the elusive puck in the reed arena
where the ice as fast as silver glass was grained
with the scraping of our skates and Sherwood sticks
as we shot toward the rubber boot goal. It was so near, so far
as in the spell of the last winter we could not break.

Rowntree Mills Park

I remember in the Rowntree photograph the house
that overlooked the swift torrents of Hurricane Hazel.
Now I'm looking for signs of the house
that Joseph, the miller,
built for his family in the 1840's.
Below the roadway I follow this overgrown path
to the point where the house should be,
but there are only a few white stones
in the shape of a broken circle.

Farther along a square shaped stone lies
like a book in the earth.
The clear-etched stone points
to a fallen trunk, torn muscle striations,
a tree which may have sheltered the house.

Stop. Think. This is the place,
smaller trees in the clearing overlooked by taller.
This is the house that Joseph Rowntree built;
the cornerstone he would have proudly set
at the ravine's edge overlooking the Humber.
Near a splintered trunk I kneel,
uncover a straight-edged stone
feel this stone, bone smooth
pull away clinging moss
tough sinews, rough roots,
this toughened old brick.

I walk to the edge of the promontory
look across the river to the other bank,
to the line of mill workers' shacks
and I hear the saw tearing wood
at the lumber mill in North York.

At the grist mill on the Etobicoke side
I can hear the paddling of the water
rushing through the mill course,
the regular sweeping rhythm of the wheel
and the turning levers and gears
at five in the morning.
I can imagine the flour rising through the moonlight
as the massive Lawder brothers heave
the barrels out into the waiting wagon,
hauling them down the rough clacking boards of Albion,
dreaming of the barmaids at the Peacock Tavern,
the barrels of whiskey at the end of the day.

My fingers dig among dried foliage and torn roots,
feel a twisted old ribbon of rusted metal,
a rim of one of the flour barrels.
Digging deeper I find another metal scrap
a twisted water pipe from the house,
along with the broken bottles of teenagers
who partied on these hidden foundations.

On the Way to Lindsay

1

Turn from the ramp to Toronto
and drive out toward Lindsay
to find the last Devins of Emery:
the direct descendant of Abraham and Isaac.
"Ray has the station sign," Marion Rowntree had said.

Through the ruins of farm machinery
the wind whines, blowing tumbleweed
across the Wagon Wheel Barn Dance Hall.
In the red Ford pickup he sits still,
his beard rugged and silver-flecked.
In the rough contours of his face
I see the Devins' lumbermen, blacksmiths, wagon makers.
"Been trying to shoot some deer this morning,"
he says, shifting his rifle over the gears.

2

"The Devins' book is wrong.
My mother didn't want anything to do with it.
Look inside the chest and bring me the blue box."
On the table I open it to the collection of war medals.
One of them a service medal from 1914-18
for "Home and Country"
a German Iron Cross
the Royal Canadian Dragoons decoration.
"There, Dad's medal of honour, right there."
"No," says Annis. "It's an essay prize for your mother, 1917."

One by one I touch the artefacts on the Devins' shelf:
the sharp blade of his father's bayonet,
his Uncle Roy's bootjack and spurs,

the refinished powder horn from Pennsylvania.
I recall Simeon dying in his tent after Queenston Heights,
John Chapman lying in the Toronto Jail after the Rebellion,
Levi's grandsons dying for the north in the Civil War.

"Do you have the Emery Railway Station sign?"
"Whatever we have is out in the Wagon Barn."
Annis leads me through the windswept yard,
across the grain of the deserted dance floor
past the dumb turntables of the old recording studio
as the sweet dry smell of wheat hangs in the air,
into the darkness of the barn
where light flashes onto a hundred broken artefacts,
                                a museum storehouse.

Through the furniture we sift,
open the carriage maker's chest of shining tools—
these the tools John Devins employed
to make the first Studebaker.
Annis uncovers an old commode,
        "There it is. The sorting box of the Emery Post Office."
I look for lost letters of the Rowntrees and the Castators,
some letter that Jennie Gillis might have left behind
for Jim Macdonald or Pearl Usher,
but find only a mousetrap, old fuses,
            and a census in French and English for 1901.

There is no railway sign and I feel disappointed.
What remains of the Devins' and Emery's past
in the wagon barn
are old barley rakes, wooden wheels, worn saddles,
old tusks from an illustration of *King Solomon's Mines*,
the coloured drawings of Annis Saunders.

Listen, I can hear the wind sifting the dust,
the rustling and jostling of couples
on Saturday nights, country and western dancing

singing of lost and found loves.
These are all the signs of Emery
broken, and in their brokenness, whole.

                    3

Annis leaves for the kitchen
while Ray leans over from his wheelchair.
"I used to steal kisses from the girls under the elms.
Many of the girls in Emery I had
under the tall elms or out in the apple orchard
where I had a pup tent.
Don't ask who they were.
There are some things a man doesn't tell."

Beyond Borders
(2000)

Passing Through Customs

If you can understand the difficulty
of traversing customs
and the questions
"Where are you from?"
"Where are you going?"
as you wait in the drizzling rain
for the train to move on,
then you can cross the tracks into another country.

If you can move beyond
the sensations of your skin,
the hard edges of your mind,
into some wilder, dangerous terrain,
and if you can permanently break
with your old physical idea of order
to see the weaving grasses,
then you can navigate these streets
and head out into open country.

If you can move beyond
the politics of blood,
and the tyranny of signs,
and if you can break
with what you consider taste
and touch the rain as if it were your thought,
then you can move into that other country.

If you can get beyond
the idea of borders,
pass through these customs,
then you would discover
the integrity of bridges,
the originality of streams,
the fecundity of ponds,

and you would move
among the enduring mountains
through the valley that holds countries together.

Driving to Fort Kent in a Mid-Spring Snowfall

I stand in the office of Sullivan's Esso Station.
"Now is the winter of our discontent."
Through customs and Fraser's whirling steam I drive.
How can I romanticize this snow
smothering the ground in silicon dust,
obscuring the Madawaska Masonry dragon?
We are ready for spring,
the fields are laid out in long symmetrical folds.
Red tractors wait outside of barn doors;
a convoy of ducks patrols the open pond.
Mid-April, once more, I am driving through Frenchville.

I curse the whine of snow on my tires.
I've had enough of these unending drives
where white fungus clings to freezing trees.
The snow falls continuously,
a sentence with no parole.
Frenchville is endless:
grain towers, potato factories, empty cabooses.

Snow falls with *les mots inconnus*
on the daily specials of roadside eateries
at the border of Frenchville.
La neige, c'est toujours comme ça:
les flocons, le givre, la rivière, tout devient vert,
étrange rêve, le brouillard sur l'eau monte
et là au-delà de la rive soudainement,
à travers le brouillard, les vieilles maisons fermées,
comme les châteaux qui s'éteignent dans la brume,
se retirent comme un langage
dans l'étincelle des yeux, la lumière de l'histoire,
le temps passe, la langue, longtemps, long time ago.

Suddenly, the river breathes a green light,
mammoth icebergs piled high in pantheon ruins
along the banks *et la neige continue,*
l'éblouissement des flocons.
Out along the grand prix raceway, I sing
la vitesse du présent: l'autre langue, les mots connus
et les rythmes subtils de la langue,
les champs nus, doux brillent dans la lumière,
les sons sont différents et je commence à chanter
dans les étranges *mers de flocons, et toutes*
les choses deviennent métaphore et flottent
dans la rivière de l'imagination.
Ici il y a le rythme de l'auto,
le rythme du piano,
le rythme du chemin
qui suit les champs, les collines
et suit à certaine distance de la rivière …

C'est la langue des ancêtres du Maine.
C'est comme un rêve, ces mots étranges
qui chantent comme les flocons.
Then ahead "Welcome to Historic Fort Kent":
The Blockhouse, The Sportsman's Paradise, The Optimist Club.
The spell of the snow is over.
I enter the town humming
the bars of a song from Île d'Orléans
Quarante-deux milles de choses tranquilles …

Poems at Hoagies

for Paul Hedeen

Not an Acadian paradise by any means,
but this August afternoon
we pore over old poems,
breathing their lives,
alchemizing experience.
Paul, as you read, your voice mingles
with the rippling voice of the waitress,
the laughter of girls on holidays,
jaunty farm boys ordering sodas.
I hear your words echo through
the ruined château of the old mill,
the dusty railway station
(now the Fort Kent Historical Museum).
In Daigle's pet store the large plumed parrot
squawks out of his Amazonian memory.
Down the road in the Acadian paradise
Doris carries out her "lumberjack special,"
bringing the news of the world to the Valley,
her voice gravelly as rapids running through pebbles.
You speak of the land of Wisconsin,
seeing a childhood girlfriend in a forest clearing.

It is out of this exile we write our songs,
when the poem suddenly centres us
and flows out past the large windows,
opening onto the river where the blurred sunlight
shimmers on the wet rocks,
and purple flowers cluster.
We watch the men on Fish River
cleanly casting their lines.

"Would you like anything else?"
asks the waitress.
No, only this window,
the last afternoon coffee,
                    lines breaking clear.

The Garden in the Rock

Slowly the garden has grown,
and so has the rock.
This year, I clear the weeds from its slopes
and see how roughly-hewn it is,
how fine the layered schist.
On its terraces my son plants portulaca
and red, shade-tolerant impatiens.
I clear the rock around the raspberry bush,
finding subtle shades of colour,
uncovering the dried lichen,
feeling the rock's form as my skin.
I am changed by this rock;
geography is what I touch in my garden,
where I hold the rock and sculpt with a trowel.

La Roche du Calvaire

In the meadow the morning is still.
The path leads to the summit of *Le Calvaire,*
no prospect of the city—
only a mowed plateau and a brown squat building
locked up with a rusted steel chain,
distant insistent drops of water
trapped in a well.

I walk until the path becomes a track,
a circular pattern of thought within my brain.
No skulls among these cold grey stones.
Everything is in ruins:
the trunks of trees ripped from the earth
in a jangled ganglia of roots,
the wire torn from strewn concrete blocks,
a foundation buried under parched grass.
The forest walls me in.

Bending to the earth,
I pick up a piece of the base rock,
carve in a clear white arc,
draw the mountain's shape,
then scrape my own initials.

I see the shoreline contours in the rock
breaking in waves beneath the face of the earth.
The earth is not a floor at all:
its runnels are worn from the rain.
On these moist stones I carefully walk
as they conform to my running shoes.

There, the leaves' veil is rent by a chink of light.
Beyond the forest is the city.
Is it important why this place is named *Le Calvaire?*
The mind makes the mountain what it is to be.

Lac Temiscouata

1 The Lake

On the ridge, I stopped to watch
a wave of cold white light moving on the water.
I wanted to go into the woods,
but that late September day
the water called to us.
And so we took the canoe out on Temiscouata
where black smooth swells rose.
Something called in the dark rising and falling of water,
in the wind moving between the slopes of the dark mountains.
There was danger in that wind
and in the swell and coldness of that water.
Our direction was not right
as we turned into the waves at a sharp angle.
What were we doing out on the water
today in this small canoe?
I wanted to store some warmth in my memory
that I could draw as a source on cold blizzard days.

2 The Forest Path

I wanted to go into as a way of going into myself,
to find something that would shine into my darkness,
an idea from a poem of Basho's I had read.
    To understand the pine
I had to become the pine,
               but where was that pine?

I followed the white path
going into the darkness that was myself,
following it as a means to a moment,
while you explained
the difference between balsam fir and pine

by picking needles from the branch.
Rubbing your fingers up and down
until the needles wore off in your hands—
the essence.

We followed the rocks to the tower,
followed their uneven forms of their waves
from some fiery upheaval eons ago.
"This is schist, *a phylo silica*."
It gleamed as I touched it,
and the sound itself, *philo,* love.
These rocks were *feuilles,*
tabula rasa, a prehistoric clay I could write on—
these lichens and moss, words
grew out of fissures
created a new earth.

3 The Tower

This place has a wider vision of the afternoon.
I have to hear my voice—
let it go.
I think of your wife, Lin,
her face silent as stone.
I said I was looking for Basho's tree.
I wanted to be a tree.
I wanted to be in the sunlight.
She said I looked younger
and her face lit up.
For a few moments the stone melted.

4 The Pine

I am looking for a tree, as Basho suggested
from this tower at the edge of Lake Temiscouata
across from the last great crouchings of the Appalachians.

Directly in front of me I see the great white pine
reaching up into the sky,
the tree is almost one with the light.

I feel the light and wind move through my limbs.
How good is the feeling of the wind on my needles,
to feel the growth at my needle tips,
to rise here into the great span of the sky,
into the curve of the afternoon.

I see a hawk ride the air currents,
I think of the hawk I treasured as a youth
at the boundary of the country and city.
It glides, knowing how to use the currents of air.
If my own lines could glide as thought
and ride the air up and crest, then
dip down into the rhythm of freedom.

5 The Cave

I am alone.
At the bend in the path I climb down, stop
where a pine tree has fallen and a large rodent
has burrowed a den.
The roots have snapped from the earth
and lichens have become ghosts.
The pine grown out of stone
could not sustain itself.
I could almost climb into this hole
to touch the roots that turn slowly to stone.

6 Shoreline

I go to the water's edge,
to the beginning of life,
and bend down to rub the rock against my chin.

It is wrinkled like the fissures of my face.
I love the texture of this rock,
the way the water engulfs me in its spray,
in its swirling and teeming around the rock
in greens, greys, and golds.
I remember the sea coast
where I went fishing on the rocks with my father.
I love the dark water crackling in the tide
in the valley of the mother rock,
                    feeding the limbs of the earth ...

The Woman in the Picture

There is a woman standing before a bookcase.
The woman is standing on the designs of a Mexican carpet,
relaxed, with her hand leaning on the case
almost as if it were a living thing.
Behind her, silhouettes of two lovers embrace.
Her eyes are closed. She is thinking
of the lake beyond the oval window.
She is now outside standing on a shore by the lake,
waking up out of this winter landscape,
opening her fingers onto the curve of the hill.
Her thoughts are clear, relaxed, simply of the world.

La Dentellière

Bent over your lace,
everything in your body
draws me toward your hands;
I can feel the tension
as you pull the two strands of thread.

The way you bend is your inclination
to thread the form of fabric.
Your cheeks and hidden smile
(if it is a smile at all)
are directed to the point in the sewing of the blue cloth.

So I observe you concentrating
on the point of that pattern you make.
I feel the motion of your hands, forearms, shoulders
threading your life,
forgetting about children, family, history
weaving them through your hands.

How Vermeer has poised your eloquent fingers,
your needle suspended in perfect tension.
I look at you in that gold and white dress;
the blue fabric is so tactile,
I could run my finger over it.
Lacemaker, you spin fabric out of yourself,
draw me into the flowers of the sun
as you float there
alive to the graceful interaction of work and life ...

The Forest is Not a Forest

In the beginning I disliked these mountains
for keeping the world out.
Now when I walk
I follow the timber-cut roadway,
and the path becomes the poem.
I see stories in the stones.
Poplar, maple, fir, pine
speak of something in the wind.

        Then the rock suddenly rises
into ridges, step by step.
      I climb over the deposits,
read the scraping on a lost school slate:
wave, vein, thrust of fire.
And the wind billows through leaves like sails
jarring my mooring from the world,
releasing me from prison
as if something in me leaps out—
a light, an abandonment
            to fuse with this wind.
Rise on the waves of air like that raven there
and survey the landscape from above,
veering over old surveyors, lost lumber camps,
old crockery and broken axes,
frayed sheets of love letters,
and so I would skirt the wind
and rise out over the border of the river.

I step into the clearing
     among the rocks, goldenrod, and Queen Anne's lace
and in that space a task challenges me
to see the power in love,
to look back and view the obstacles in the road
as the necessary things to come through.

Here is a madness, a holding
onto the self, being separate
from the world. Pick up
that piece of rock there
                    and throw it down into dust.

Break the self,
                    and walk only here
as if someone else,
                    as if I were that beech
   or that raven still riding out there ...
Give up this separate boundary
and learn just to be the feeling,
the flight of the raven,
                    the line of the sea in the rock
or the colour slowly suffusing from the season.
Learn to uncover these things
and step out onto the edge
of that round rock where the world glimmers
dangerously in its fierce purity.
Here lose your name and names:
horned snail, red lantern berries, shadowy fragrant ferns.

Walk now on the path,
as if the stones were allegories
of a life that is not yours.
Discover it as you go on
in this lightness of the falling rain
where the sky touches your forehead,
and you feel the dreams of the dog.
Go ahead—
say it isn't so:
                    the forest is not a forest.

Riding the SMT Down the Appalachian Route on a Late October Afternoon

Already the roofs of the houses are covered in snow,
yet as we head south it begins to disappear.
Rocks shine on exposed gravel beds;
mountain slopes extend to the river.
Synclines and anticlines
don't follow the highway's irregular course.
Here are the Appalachians,
distant humped mountains gathered together.

How small is our presence on their slopes:
houses hugging the hillsides,
pumpkins grinning from sagging porches,
porcelain dolls for sale at a swamp's edge,
a slogan for the politician who saved the country—
even the longest covered bridge in the world.

The gorges cut through the mountain
take us back to a time long before billboards.
The landscape is a long-playing movie;
on the horizon the sunlight projects
its blue beams onto the furrows of farmers' fields
which follow the larger form of the hills.

Now, gradually it's getting dark.
I'm falling into sleep
to the music of the humming tires,
the percussion of the wind against the window frame.
I'm gazing into the reflection of the afternoon
riding into the mountain ridge.
We move through the woods following
the banks, hills, dips, and we rise
to meet the dark fold,
up into the wild
and down into the gorge.

We follow the ridge flowing
as if we were suspended,
and it is travelling through us.

Then the ridge suddenly falls
into the wide forms of sand pits,
where men are digging with diesel shovels,
thick layers of sand and gravel. Slowly
they hollow out glacial deposits,
thousands of years ago,
carving out the walls.
The bus glides down the hill along the Saint John
until there is no road,
only water on both sides drifting by
                          the ancient backgrounds.

Shortcut Through the Renous

Even before I came to New Brunswick
the mover had spoken of its curves and twists,
"impossible to drive in winter."
One October I tried driving it—
vans and cars loading at the gas station.
Turbulent clouds gathered
and ten minutes in
winter swept over us,
blinding the roads.

Already I can see the green halo of growth,
the beginning chlorophyll, a purplish breath
announcing leaves, birches shedding
scrolls of skin-tinted bark.
Drive over the hill, the black
open stream. Put on the brakes. Stop.
Outside, sounds are everywhere.
The snow is protean
as molecular bonds break, ice rising
in the wavering steam.
There is splash in the ebony water;
the brown ribbed-bottom ripples,
a slithering of mud things.
Trout swim below phosphorescent ceilings of ice.
Slime speckles the surface, a green cauliflower.

On this bridge's edge, a board
is exposed, the faded texture of an old railway tie.
I need this spring:
this dark inlet is a door.
Learn to let go
of the heart's driftwood.
Listen, the voices of clarity—
blue jays, orioles.

By the bridge, clear brown water
flows through the melting ice,
through the fissure of winter
from a deep, quiet opening.

The Gorge

We pass over the black turmoil of water,
the churning of turbines.
The waters thunder under Grand Falls.
Six years it took to tunnel through this rock.
The launch's engine splutters
as geographers eat their lunches quietly
and study these high cliffs.
Here the French explorer would
have gazed upon these cliffs,
the grandeur of the New World.

Slowly we turn into the silence of the gorge
where a cormorant skirrs over dark water.
After examining railways, lumber yards, bridges
we enter the rugged Ordovician age,
the black river winding among these rocks
as it has for millions of years.

On the bas-relief of these rocks
are scrolled parabolas of mediaeval domes, cupolas,
and flying buttresses
carved out of a cliff.
Imagine their genesis, the veins
ribboned in chalk, fire creating an action painting
for the ages. The lines throw us
back to the forging of minerals.

Passing through this prehistoric canyon
we feel transient.
The captain names the rocks:
      "The Camel's Back"
            "Indian Head"
                  "The Sphinx,"
                        "The Pulpit Rock."

These rocks could be the Giant's Causeway in Antrim,
Peruvian mountain crags
where Incan temples rose into mist.
The water swirls through the whirlpools,
and the gravelly voices mingle with our own.
Here, the Saint John is so narrow,
I can almost touch the gorge walls with my hands.

I want this gorge to be inviolable,
separate from the human, as natural
as the eagle's flight.
I want its geology to be invulnerable
in its immaculate, enduring forms,
untouchable as the myth of Malobiannah
the woman who sacrificed herself for her tribe
or the 19th century funambulist
who crossed the thundering falls.
I want to separate the rock from the human,
to see its powerful continuing forms.

Mountain Garden

for Audrey Côté St-Onge

Sitting on your porch I look up at terraced gardens
where tulips and daffodils waver in a windy chorus.
There was nothing here
until you planted the flowers and built walls,
shaping the garden into an amphitheatre.

Inside your house are paintings:
a field of dancing wheat
blowing about as the waves on Fundy
          your painting of childhood fields,
the farm at Rivière Verte—
            strawberries rising to defy the gravity of time.
In your studio is a still life:
the green opaque bottle
holds one lush red poppy
against a green-yellow background—
golden brown sunflowers drying
so that they rise off the page,
dials of thick bronze mandalas.

On the easel is the painting of birches.
Trying to get the atmosphere right,
you erase textures of sky.
You etch the rocks in your garden.
Now they glisten with light in ridges,
            in scratches, veins.
The moss with pink lanterns
lightens the miracle of lichens,
minutiae of living under the surface of things.

Light grows out of the darkness.
You lighten the bark of trees
until it almost fades into the form of sky
where the birches stream upward
into the smoky-blue lines of twilight.

La Fenêtre

Il y a des après-midi
où le givre fait des formes
comme les mythes de l'orfèvre
les symboles sculptent en glace
les dauphins, les châteaux
les graines comme le sable
l'écume éclate ,
les étoiles scintillent,
la forme d'écriture,
les lettres de Stendhal.

Il y a des soirées comme celle-ci
calmes et chaudes
quand la rivière respire le brouillard,
et obscurcit les contours précis de pays différents,
et soudainement la brume coule
sur La Roche du Calvaire comme un volcan
vous pensez à votre père, le raconteur
qui fait des contes de fées
sur une île dans les Caraïbes.

Et doucement, la nuit vient
et les lanternes apparaissent
comme les bijoux d'une guirlande
sur les courbes du pont
et scintillent comme les étoiles
et obscurcit le miroir de la Madawaska
(on oublie la fumée du moulin Fraser)
et dans cet encadrement
la fenêtre devient une carte postale
dans les lettres écrites en or
commes l'atmosphère douce
Edmundston by night
et les mots suspendent la nuit
dans cette étrange saison hivernale.

Lighthouse

Wind tugs at the mosquito net,
and out on the bay
the moon shines coldly over Île Bonaventure;
a thousand thronging birds begin to settle for the night,
only a few stragglers gliding over the waves toward the cliff.

The lighthouse spreads its beacon across the waters
over the years of shipwrecks and their legends.
I take a gulp of wine;
there the surge of the sea,
the moon, the island and the lighthouse,
a stage set for our separate human destinies.

This afternoon in our Datsun 510 we struggled up Gargantua,
only to find the campground full,
overheard a Rabelaisian laughter on the summit.
Now we pitch our tent in an overflow field,
warm palms over barbecue coals,
feel wind blow across waves and tall grasses.

I lift the bottle toward the stars.
It is good to be near the sea again.
I salute the constellations
and think of the journeys yet to make.
The beacon flickers over
the dark bow of cargo freighters.

Take another sip and feel the warmth.
Is this not what we wanted?
—a fire, the sea, even the cold wind
awakening us to the never ending realities of space,
as we work out the pattern of our lives under the zodiac.

How good this red wine is.
Beyond us lies a lone white house,
The Three Sisters and Percé,
green waves rolling through the archway
separating it from the mainland.

Here under the shadow of Gargantua,
the earth folded from an upheaval of force.
We camp at the edge of the continent,
looking out at the slow circling light,
think of our future as we watch
the last white birds gliding toward the cliffs of Île Bonaventure.

Ghost Town

Sunday is cold and dark.
Wind sweeps blackboard sky over desolate water,
children shout, dogs run.
Grouard's church leans into the wind,
strong as the Bishop's fingers
that trimmed red-veined beams and drew burning hearts.
The people named the town after him.
When he died, they torched his residence.

You speak of Ghost-Pipe who married
a crippled girl and when she died, he searched
for her in the Land of the Dead.
The path narrows to a gate sign
where I trace worn words:

>   This Place Holy Ground
>   Do Not Play Here

Plastic flowers cover gravestones:
a photograph of a fisherman,
a boy killed in a car crash,
a lance corporal who died of a coronary,
four children in the flu epidemic of 1918.

The grass reaches our waist.
We stumble into trenches,
cannot tell grass from grave.

Ghosts sing of the last night:
        reckless boys
                rebellious girls
            lonely priests
                    forgotten soldiers.

Twilight sky turns slowly into darkness.
We stand on the edge of the glassy world
where prospectors once travelled north
                              along the Heart River.
Ghost-Pipe's wife returned
                        to the Land of the Dead.
The Bishop's stories
            buried in the legends of these tombs.

Still, dogs run
        bark crazily before the street's façade.
Children spin on their bicycles.
Darkness ebbs over the ridge,
                over the great expanse of glowing nothing.

Aunt Cornelia

Of course, you went by other names:
Corrie, Connie and *Tante Cockie*.
Christmas mornings, you owned the bathroom on Habitant Drive,
emerging two hours later as Queen Nefertiti,
your gleaming body wrapped in a C.P. hotel towel,
hair bound in a swirling turban,
eyebrows singed into perfect accent circonflexes.

We heard rumours of imminent marriages—
the reporter at *The Globe and Mail* who wrestled a bear,
some wealthy businessman or other in Europe,
a millionaire cattle rancher in Texas—
but the engagements were inevitably broken.
And you would suddenly appear for a whirlwind visit,
carrying more souvenir towels from Mexico or Spain.

Your elocution was perfect, as if you were auditioning,
only the faintest quiver of a Dutch accent.
You lived as a high-class model at the Royal York Hotel,
and when we visited, you had our snacks sent up by room service.
Later in an perfumed apartment in Rosedale
your bedroom was decorated with Venetian canals
and souvenirs of matadors in Mexico City.
Above your bed, the embossed velvet legends of Hiawatha
surrounded by deer with moist-eyed deer.

You became friends with "our pet, Juliette,"
and Rutenberg at Holt and Renfrew.
You once caught T.B., which you got over,
but you never got over Canadian winters.
So you flew to California, opened a boutique
and served Doris Day and other movie stars.

Word finally reached us that you were marrying
a wealthy Hungarian engineer—the nephew of Zsa Zsa Gabor.
Your brother, Herman, visited you in Los Angeles,
had to catch your chimpanzee on a neighbour's balcony.
Later, your husband went crazy from too much drinking,
and you emigrated from Santa Monica to Arizona.

These are the pictures that I have of you,
but there is one I left out: Christmas Eve, 1956,
when you and Mother made *oliebollen,* laughed
and sang Dutch songs, running
up and down the stairs, tossing
flour at each other
until it rained down,
changing you into girls.

"Tear Off Your Yellow Star"

"My children, Alexander and Fenna, where are you?
Look around at us
being taken away in cattle cars—
the gas chambers are not rumours.
Tomorrow we're being shipped to Westerbork.
My mother and brother are already
on their way to Auschwitz.
How many of us are left?
There by the fence, raspberries.
Ben, when was the last time you ate raspberries?
They're delicious.
I'm ripping off my yellow star."
"Gerrit, leave the star. They'll kill you."
"Not if we walk now.
The guards are down the line.
Tear off your yellow star.
Let's go for a walk."

Years later, he remembered that night:
Ben and he walked on the edge of the gravel,
away from the death camp
in the direction of the *Zuider Zee*
until his shoes grew ragged and
darkness erased the path.

Geel War Cemetery, Belgium

At the gate an old man with a scarred face
speaks in a language I do not understand
and guides me to the register of soldiers.
Through the pages I search for you,
great-uncle for whom I am named.
You served in the British Second Army
fought in the battle of the Meuse-Escaut Canal.

When I was on the phone overlooking the runway
at Pearson International Airport last year,
Father told me how you climbed out of a foxhole
to drag a wounded comrade to safety,
but as you reached for him
a bullet pierced your brain.

You may have died on a day like today,
that last morning sipping coffee,
writing a letter to your wife and daughter,
recalling a furlough in Piccadilly Circus.
Already you hear gunfire
beyond the river that you would not cross.

At the end of row D, I find your gravestone,
with a shamrock and the motto QUIS SEPARABIT
L. Hutchman, Irish Guards, 14 September, 1944.
All goes on in the world as it has before:
the church bells peel for evening service,
the rooster crows in the field,
the persistent sound of mourning doves,
purple roses grow by the barbed-wire fence,
the old farmer digs up weeds in the garden
as he did fifty years ago under the sound of gunfire.

It is my sadness at seeing not only your grave,
but so many other graves
with inscriptions from the Bible and the Torah,
men scarcely in their twenties.
I cannot read many of them.
I am alone. The wind is cold.

Wild Irish guardsman,
I place a purple rose under your name.
The old man is waiting by the gate.
His son and daughter-in-law stand impatiently;
he draws me a map to the Geel railway station.
He knows why I am here.

Reading the Water
(2008)

Swimming Toward the Sun

I could not stay in the cabin.
Others slept while I stepped
out under the night sky.
How cold and damp the air.
Before me is the lake.
I walk down to the rock.
I think of those who died this year.
The lake is dark, heavy, cloudy.
There is mist on the lake
curling like grief.

I sit on the beach
listen to the frogs
in the large pit of the lake
singing in tenor and bass,
syncopated in time,
then the loons
blowing their mysterious horns
to other loons who answer them,
and the Phoebes who raise their little melodies
while large invisible fish splash like timpani.
The sounds rise and fall in this pastoral,
an orchestra in the morning mist.

I swim away from the dock;
the sun begins to break
the horizon. I swim toward it
as it sends golden rays across
the waves, and two loons
glide through serenity.
They disappear into the light
as I swim through.

Listening

This morning, over the water
a voice in the light is calling,
Star of Venus, never brighter,
a goblet in the water.
I go to the edge of the lake,
gaze over the water to the pine trees
shrouded in their fuzzy coats,
blurred against the final light of the stars.

The light, like blood, bevels on the water
over the folds of its dark body.
Here the birds call
out to one another in their unctuous cries.
Their ululating gullets, yodelling the air,
bring movement to the pines
in the nightclub of the forest.

I am discontent.
I leave this old self,
a snake skin, on the rock.
I call out to the ghosts of the past.
I call out to the wound on the water,
but the lake, a balm,
draws my voice down into its darkness.

Forget your adolescence.
Give voice to your pain.
Listen, now, to the birds trilling—
come closer, closer
little bird, breathe on me,
bring delight in the rustling of your wings.

On the sandbank
by the water
that shell, mother of pearl,
fading crescent moon,
a quiet ear listening.
Shed your old skin.
Listen to the water,
to the light.
Here, on the shore,
listen to the bristling music of birds,
the voices of morning.

Loon

This morning I see you
out on the water,
your long neck quilted with stars,
treading darkness, like a swan.
Why did we stamp you
on the dull gold of our dollar
and christen you "loony."
It was a name kids called each other
on the school bus. Loon.
I think of you along with the moon,
la lune, lunacy of lovers.
How far are we
from your gliding
through darkness?
Yet, when you call out
a sound not human, not made by cello
or bassoon, just a sound which suddenly
shapes the hills, granite, pine,
something in us goes out to search for
home.

Flight of the Luna Moth

As we wander along the path, in the branches we see a lunar moth flying up toward the purple halo of the glass lamp, trying to get closer to its dream, moving from tree to tree like a child playing hide and seek in the darkness.

We follow its graceful dance as it scores the air, tracing its movements like a luminous thread, tying pieces of moments together, like the scenes of a story teller. In awe we follow the dollop of its flight, until landing.

Six-year-old Elizabeth brings me the lunar moth in her hand. I notice it with its two magenta-bordered wings outspread, still breathing from its white-cocooned belly. Later, I see the outline of a wing in the woodchips. I bend over and find one single wing, soft as down.

Climbing Mount Boyce

The pathway is not clear
as we move up *Burned Trail* onto *Lone Pine*.
There is no need to reach the summit.
Perhaps on these lower slopes
we will find a place where the forest opens out.

We can hear the invisible river,
the flow from the waterfall.
It is the way I see life, moving toward an end,
a place where I can see my life.
According to Schopenhauer's writing—
if you live long enough and climb high enough,
you can see your life like the pages of a novel.

I want to make something more
out of this walk, to find the moment, breaking
over the horizon, like that recent afternoon
behind the Pitti Palace in the Boboli Gardens
where we climbed in nearly forty-degree heat.

The sound of the stream becomes stronger.
We can taste the coolness in the air.
Among the black chiselled rocks, under
the grasses and the branches—
the waterfall.

It is not what I expected,
not the waterfall the woman told us about,
just a stream falling through
the shiny rocks.
I get down to face the rocks and push
the bottle into that smallest stream.

Perhaps death
will come like this, not with the vista, but
the closeness of nature,
the tingling of consciousness,
the fullness of berries and mushrooms,
each turning in the path among the arrangement of rocks,
the high trees bending, whispering
like water in the calls of birds. And you will see

the whole contour of the mountainside above
you could not see before,
and below the way you had come.
Each moment changing place with the other.

Fred Cogswell

When I see you lying in bed,
the bruises on your arms,
I'm aware of the resilience of your body,
the strong light in your eyes,
those fingers, with the strength of a farm boy,
that have written so many books.

You loved sports, running two miles
back to school to play baseball after dinner,
sinking a basket in that championship game.
Your grandmother from Bouctouche
instilled the love of French in you.

You loved to chase butterflies,
devoured the Old Testament and the New Testament,
the *Anglo-Saxon Chronicle*,
any novel you could get your hands on,
then poetry, which became your life.

You came from Centreville, made it larger,
like the eagle that glides over the Saint John Valley
tracing ever farther flights.
When you wrote, how carefully you painted
the portraits of the villagers, like an old Dutch master
faithful to their character.

The philosophy in your poems
was one that does not divide the world into separate
things, but reveals life as darkness and light,
the crescent of the moon
and the corona of the sun.

Now in your last struggle
you follow the path from the farmhouse
through the apple orchard down by the cedars and
the creek, out toward the big rock pile under the tree
where you can see beyond the circumference of the mountains.

Waterfall in the Woods above Simeonovo

Why is it that waterfalls
are so different
here in the woods
overlooking Sofia?
I sit on the large rock,
listening as the noise of water
fills the air like the song
of rising birds.
Why is it that the river
sounds like rain rushing
through the rocks like wild horses?
Here the water falls from
two different streams,
down into different
waterfalls. It creates colours:
grey, blue, green
in a turbulence of white—
lines move into the colour of sound.
The two streams are from different
places, like thoughts
from opposite sides of the brain
that come together, singing.

The Cave

As we climb the tortuous path,
work our way along the staggered
pattern of rocks, a natural way
for stubborn pilgrims,
Svetla reminds us,
"You must pass through the centre of the circle"
(at least this was suggested for sinners).

The uneven white steps lead into
the darkness of the cave. This is where
Ivan of Rila survived seven years
through the freezing winters
and the heat spells of summer.
I imagine his meagre existence
in the rocky furnishings
of this cave, the darkness
and his silence next to God.

I edge slowly along the dark passageway.
it is difficult to climb its rough-smooth
surfaces. Suddenly I stare into the stark
face of a saint, the amber glimmer of a candle
and I venture beyond the glow,
the oblique cracks of the rock's roof
close in on me.

The cave comes to a dead end.
I slip,
grip the wet rib of a rock.
The darkness grows
and the cave narrows.
I hear voices echoing from ahead.
I decide to follow them.

I creep like a bear along these ledges,
and my eyes look up to
a bubble of light where the sky peeks
in. But how to climb this steep wall ...
when out of the rocks the steps of a ladder
appear. To the top rung I climb.
The voices are gone.
I place my palms on the edge of the round rock—
the opening is too small—
and force myself toward the aperture.
Without thinking further, I climb,
my knapsack pressed against the rock.
As I lift myself,
feel my hands on the edge of the earth,
I find myself on the path once again.

Lust

Have you ever really thought of the word? Lust. A scrabble of the libido. Let the word roll on your tongue. The long "l" is a liquid, curving thigh. The "u" has the rich taste of a sexual vowel, and the ending "st," a closing of the lips.

Rhyme the word "lust," with "bust." Yes it doubles. "Must" is that inevitability of desire—turn it around and there's a hidden "slut." Or there is "tusl," that ultimate tussle with nocturnal fantasies. Lust. It's more than the word—a desire that is in us, between the goalposts of the "l" and the "t."

How is it language gives rise to lust? Say the words. Imagine them through the negligée of language: the amber moonshine, the midnight delta, the hidden harbour, the lighthouse, the peninsula in light—geography of desire.

Developing

Father worked in a darkroom at Kodak,
his work mysterious as atomic physics.
Sometimes I took a negative out of the box,
held it up to the sun
to identify my parents, my sisters, myself,
foreigners in a dark geography.

Father had his own lab at home,
a sunless spare room
where he had an enlarger, slid
the negatives under an electric eye,
clicked the x-ray machine
where the glossy paper slowly changed—
the acceleration of the cotyledons' growth,
as in a grade eight science class.

I would watch him dip
the paper into a chemical bath, move
it slowly back and forth
as if he were washing a sheet in a river,
unrolling it like a scroll
in pungent hypo solution where light
broke through—
first shapes emerging from the sea.

Paper glimmered under infrared bulbs.
He was barely able to see,
the solitary light of his eyes
was focused on his fingers
with their knowledge of the dark.
I saw the first elementary forms: the birth cells,
the dance of chromosomes,
messenger RNA.
Out of these shells, curves and designs
the familiar faces slowly appeared.

This ritual he performed
every night in the factory.
I develop these images
within the dark template of myself.

The Shell

You look out at me from brown eyes like an orphan. On your skin were Japanese characters or Arabic script. Now I place you in my palm, shell, sea snail. I feel you smooth as porcelain. You are round, firm as a breast. I feel the curve of your upper ribs where you are flecked with sand pigment from the beaches where you have lain. When I turn you over you are the shape of a tiger fish. Yet, rubbing my fingers, as over braille, ribs become keys. I hear a distant music when my father, long ago on a beach in Portrush, lifted you to my ear to hear the sea gurgle and swim within your body.

And now, I am shocked, deafened and blinded by the ego of my shell. There is no sea now. I'm addressing an absence: it is not you, only myself talking. This is your marble grave. As I look within, I see what form you might have taken. I feel your softer brown-moist body, like my own, inside this carapace of being.

You are not there, only the structure of your form. I feel you in the currents, swimming among the gaudy flowers, the turbid underwater forest your species. I hear the music and taste the delicious brine, luminous, green transparent light falling from upper water—and I am loose and free as your cousin jellyfish, no longer aware of my shell, but moving through the sea so long ago.

You are not Yorick's skull in Hamlet's hand. Now you are the creature within me.

Reading the Water

I recollect weekend trips, my father following
red and yellow lines on maps
to obscure places with aboriginal names—
trips that began on forlorn bridges,
rivers that suddenly
disappeared into tangled undergrowth,
narrowed to open fields and high grasses.
He had strategies that I could only imagine
as he followed the curves of the river,
a soldier on a subversive campaign,
recalling something no doubt Mother had said,
that drove him away from his family
to these hedge-lined fields
where the water was black and rushing.
He stood in the water, hip waders against
the current and waited
for the speckled, the brown, the rainbow,
moving slowly, until
he chose the right fly, the appropriate angle.
Lassoing the line,
he cast it out into an "s" above the current,
tugging at it
jazzy improvisation
playing the waters with his fingers,
reading its bubbles as notes on some aqua score,
reading the sounds, the currents, the silences,
marks on a rippling dark page.
He waited for the change in tension.
Timing was all. The tug.
He could wait there,
wait there almost
all morning—or so it seemed,
and I followed him, continually onward,
to catch that fish.

Fishing on the River Wye

1

At the tip of the promontory I stand, casting
with my father, into the waters of Midland Bay.
He is patient. He knows where the fish swim.
I loop the line out
into the dark hollow of the water
where it is still, and wait.

Thirty years ago, long before the marina,
we rowed over a wreck with its bow
protruding out of the water, an ancient Viking hull.
In the old green rowboat my father trolled, sculled
a pathway through the insects hovering
over the yellow blossoms on lily pads.
We waited in silence as hungry seagulls thronged
and shrieked through the sun-entangled trees.

He taught me the techniques of fishing, to
cast the line like a light lasso,
unspool without entangling,
wait for the precise moment,
taut with line between thumb and index finger, wait
for the tug, then release
the line, let the fish
swim with it through the water.
A man of few words on fishing trips,
he was more adept
in his language of hooks, sinkers and lures.

Late afternoon and we stand
on this windy ridge, the sun blurred
through clouds over Christian Island.
I see the edge of an iron rib
curling over the rocks,
the old boat like a beached whale.
I had swum out to the wreck, climbing
over gunnels, slipping
down into its depths where the lime light
shone in Technicolor,
golden green weeds waving their hair like mermaids.
I had explored its hulk, the rusted bolts
the corroded sides where a bass
turned its black eye toward me and swam away.
This was as close to a fish as I would get.

He will not tell his story
straight, any more than he would
chart a course for fishing.
I watch Father concentrating
on the line, waiting
for the tug as he searches
the rising and falling
of the waves. He does not move
quickly, changes his strategy
to read the shifting wind.
He does not speak.
Beyond silence I read meaning
in his fingers, his arms, his eyes.

The Last Boat-Train on the Great Lakes

The port is empty now,
the waters clear.
There are no freight sheds,
smokestacks, gardens, ships.
There are no docks—
everything has gone back to nature.
Across the harbour the grain elevators
        and a yellow generating station stand.
Up until 1990, when the government
cancelled grain subsidies,
they were still in use.

To the edge of the cracked pier
I walk past smooth, iron hawsers
which had moored the *Keewatin* and the *Assiniboia*,
ships built on the banks of the Clyde
sailed across the Atlantic,
up the Saint Lawrence River
just three weeks before the *Titanic* sank.
They had to be sawed in half,
floated across Lake Ontario,
reassembled in Buffalo.

This is where my father,
a CPR conductor in the mid '50s,
rode up on the train
bringing passengers to the steamships
for weekend holiday cruises to Fort Arthur and Port William.

He sold Club Soda
to businessmen in swivel seats,
who mixed it with outlawed liquor.

On weekends, he waited
for their return,
fishing from the docks,
sleeping in the caboose.

Now the ships are ghosts,
pictures in souvenir books.
My father, with his 35 mm camera,
filmed the steamship with the boat-train.
We waved to the crew raising the gangplank,
looked up at the smokestack
as the foghorn bellowed—
one of the last cruises on the Great Lakes.
Beyond the docks, I remember the sign,
"One mile to Paradise Point."

Along the cinder path
in the weeds I find
a hidden imprint of tracks,
a fossil of the ties.
I push the lever of red signal
as if to change it back to
that other time, but
it's stuck.

Intensive Care

for Father

For more than a week
you have lain in this sealed ward,
a thick tube stuck in your mouth.
Your nose, bashed like a boxer's in a late round,
has dried blood across it.
Your white hair is pushed back
like an old Jewish prophet's.

You labour to breathe.
Your eyes, drugged on morphine,
stare at the ceiling, now and then
closing so slightly.
I say, "I am here."
Your eyes try to speak.
Your lips try to open, but
only quiver.

I know there are words
beyond the tubes and catheter,
residual words rising from
within the river of your being,
something of your life
that you did not say
or could not say—
and why, like a fighter,
you hold on for seven days to this life.

Irish Spring

There are certain images that remain:
the memory of walking with my uncle and father
along a chalky road somewhere in Ireland,
the sound of water falling
through rocks, running
into a stream. It is the song of a singer
whose words I do not know.
We stop, climb down
a bank, and sip from the rusty pipe.
I smell the minerals in the water.
It is the clearest, coldest water I have ever tasted.
I watch my uncle, and then my father,
drink. The thirst and the heat vanish.
We are alone in the lighted shadows
of the trees, where the wind stirs.
I listen to the stream of the earth,
the voice of the spring
becoming my own.

The Dancer, Resting

Tang Dynasty
618-907
earthenware with painted decoration

The dancer rests
her elbow on her knee.
The music has ended.
Perhaps she replays
the motion in her mind.
This is what she does,
gives herself up to motion.

The sculptor
shows her
resting,
but see the graceful
turning, how her desire is
in her limbs
contained—
see how she moves before the court
in the act of dancing.

It is in the movement of her legs
and the gestures of her arms.

She has just performed
the dance of her life,
poised in this moment of rest,
                                    and the remnants of the dance ...

Chinese Erotic Scene at the Royal Ontario Museum

After passing by the bronze horses,
vases, bowls—*lei,* suddenly
in the second century,
in the Eastern Han Dynasty,
a scene on the grey stone appears:
a man is making love to a woman
on a carpet of the forest.
A group of onlookers stands before it:
"It's a picture of a rape scene
or a prostitute, with men waiting,"
one woman cries out.
"Oh, I don't like that one!" says another.
"Let's go on to the good times."
The group is embarrassed and wants
to move on. The guide leading
the group away murmurs:
"Perhaps these are the good times."
Beside me, a professor of Chinese says,
"This work was banned in Fort Leavenworth."
It is all in grey, finely etched;
the man is about to enter the woman,
a basket and cane beside her.
Her legs slide over his shoulders,
(so long ago)
and his smaller friend behind him
slowly pushes his buttocks:
"What are friends for?" says the professor of Chinese.
And the woman's clothes dangle in the branches
in the sunlit afternoon, as the monkeys
chatter above them, peering
down, enjoying their fun,
and the peacock spreads his feathers.

It's afternoon.
The third man stands behind the tall tree
with an erection.
There is a buzz in the air.
It's late afternoon and sunny.
Perhaps this is a fertility rite or a legend.
Who knows now?
Somewhere in a warm afternoon
in the late second century AD in China.

The Terra-Cotta Warriors

They are there, what is left
of Emperor Qin Shi Huang's great army,
a testament to his power.
They are defending his city
long after his death.
They are in battle formation.
The first row of warriors has no armour,
nor do they wear helmets.
They are armed with only their bravery,
their readiness to fight.
Each figure is actual size,
modelled on a warrior,
faces tough, wise, fair.
Faces of professional soldiers
you might have seen in a bar
2,200 years ago.

Now you try to read their individual lives,
the particular lines in their faces,
row after row, restored in perfect formation.
They are in columns, separated by rows of earth.
There are four horses,
trained for battle, yet if you look farther back
you see the formation is broken,
the terra-cotta soldiers not whole, but pieces
almost as if they had died in battle,
pierced by spears, arrows from crossbows, fallen
to their knees, their bodies
decaying in the dust, in the fragments
of wheels, the dust of the wooden chariots,
the leather straps.

Once the beams of a roof protected them;
now they crumble, yet even in their destruction
we imagine their lives, their dedication.
So many things we don't know about their lives:
playing with children by the goldfish pools,
with their own little terra-cotta soldiers,
cutting the flowers in the gardens,
at home in bed with their wives,
sitting alone in the still coolness of the temple,
sipping wine with friends, waiting
for the next battle
with concern in their eyes and fear.
Perhaps, if we look beyond the mask of the soldiers,
we could see that it was not all war.
We see ourselves in them, speaking,
"We'll live beyond this battle,
live to triumph, to drink and love again."

Climbing the Great Wall

1

I walk into the guardhouse
overlooking the valleys and the mountains.
Standing here in the cool air,
by at the ancient fireplace,
I see before me young men playing cards, waiting
as the ancient guard had waited ...

We dragged in firewood
from slopes, always on the lookout for the enemy,
watching the far fires
of comrades in the distance,
waiting for the signal,
signs of the invading army.
Here, we would wait under the cold stars,
born to this soldier's life
in service of the dragon—
better than bearing stones
up mountains with donkeys.
We think of our comrades.
We tell stories of old battles,
of friends no longer here,
gone to the place of ancestors.
We play games with the emperor's dice;
it keeps us warm at night.

I think of my wife,
her body under silk,
our desire to be together.
Yet we are so solitary in the night,
only the voices of the guardhouses.

These walls are our safety—
they bind the country.
They are our way of life.
They follow the mountains.
They are the mountains.
They are the skeleton.
They are the dragons.

Sometimes, late at night under the call of eagles,
under the frosty moon, I listen
and write my thoughts down.
We are forgotten at the outpost.
We are here, guarding the country.
Remember our lives.
We could give you our names
but you would not remember them.

2

I reach the base guardhouse
and I stop, my heart racing beneath my rib cage.
"It's only 423 steps," one student says.
"Lean forward or you will fall back—
keep going."
It's as steep as a Mayan temple.
I begin the climb, step by step toward the summit.
It is harder, slower than I thought,
like moving in another element.
I hear younger people clapping,
Here I am at the summit of Mutianyu,
the wall weaves like a dragon's tail among the mountains.

I see an eagle veer out of the clouds,
its sleek white form
curves and rises in a spiral,
winding up the mountain of air.

Then another eagle joins it
and they fly, tracing circles,
skaters making figure eights
in their mutual symmetry
above the Great Wall over China.

Personal Encounters
(2014)

Pencil

You are yellow,
the colour of the evening sun,
rare as a harvest moon.
You are composed of graphite
(from the Greek, *graphein*, to write).
You are mined from the earth.
I'm writing with your carbon.

I love the sound of writing,
the way words sound,
the way they appear.
I feel the force in my fingers,
the movement like a rudder through water.
Sometimes you go almost silent
as a sigh or just move smoothly
like fingers across the lover's shoulder.

I love the action of writing,
the way I can conjure words out of the world.
When I look through the frame of the room
at the road lighted by the archipelago of light bulbs
drawn like a bracelet over the dark, snowy hillsides,
it invites me into the journey of the night
and the evening itself a mise en scene

Pencil, yours is a kingdom of rocks and earth.
Write me on this page,
write me away slowly
when the movement of the earth
takes the energy of the carbon
leaving itself on the page.

It is a moment of kinaesthesia,
electricity exploding at a molecular level,
the transfer of energy in its private metaphors,
moving me toward the horizon of the earth
beyond your end.

Li Po Remembers the Young Woman

Why do I think of Li Po
in the mountains of the gorgeous
country of the Yangtze
as he stands before the river?
The moon mirrors
the water as a reflection of his life,
with the memory of a young woman years ago.

Her lambent limbs reclined before the bamboo curtain
and beyond the rim of his wine cup
he read the pleasures of life.
Passion distilled in his older being
when she sang like the nightingale.
She looked at him with the brown pools
of her eyes, held him in the dark,
the candle burning within him.

Li Po recalls now standing before the blue ancient seas
of the moon and what he had seen and
how she made him forget the scenes of battle,
the intrigues of court,
the sudden inexplicable executions.
"Come," she said, "sip my tea, after your long journey."

Why is it that she remains on the rim of his consciousness
when he sips the moonlight of his wine
before the dark menacing waters?
Beyond the edge of the pier
he pours one more drink,
thinking of that young woman in his arms.

He tries to reach for the words
that would paint the fullness of this scene.
He slips down into the warm water,
and the moon, a porcelain dish, shatters.

Listening to Mahler's Sixth Symphony
Driving Home Through the Saint John River Valley

So many times I have heard the symphonies when
looking out across the currents of the water
and watching the bold moon, a shining goblet,
change its place.

It is the music that gathers the landscape
as it rolls along before the car
and takes me out along the dark bends
past the foxes with their torch tails running
across roads as they hold the wildness of the wind,
cows munching in their nocturnal meditation,
the barns crouched in the shelter of their hay,
the late night workers hauling logs in machines.

It is this movement of the landscape,
this rush of innocence in the music
as the configuration of notes
dances me under these evening skies
enlarging this country in the winding hills.
The moon's cosmic eye
draws me along the land
deeper into its history
into its intricate, long-suffering changes in the lives
of Aboriginals walking along these shores.

The Austrian composer opens this land
in a music that drives me deeper
into it, a music that is the river
of great spilling sounds,
the trilling of the trees
rising into space.

I listen to the music.
It is not just the events,
but the intuition of darkness of the twentieth century you foresee:
the wars, the occupations, the death camps,
something we failed to look at and confront
in the darkness that was fear.
It is in the music, this constant rising
here of the river that mirrors the music
that you write and conduct
in this struggle of the Sixth Symphony.

How difficult it is to love during war,
to turn away from darkness,
the Jewish girls who were full of life
when rounded up by Nazis in razzias.

Did I not stop, frozen in time at the border in Emmerich
watching the railway workers in those ancient orange cars,
which would have taken people to the camps?
Perhaps you saw these things, Mahler,
in your vision of armies clashing through
the streets, the cities flaming in destruction.

Mahler, we now celebrate this life in joy,
yet it is the tragedy we must face
that gives us a deeper human voice
struggling with our selfish skin.

Rainer Maria Rilke

Your mother wanted you to be a girl
and clothed you like a doll in chiffon dresses.
Your father wanted you to be a soldier in the army,
but you rebelled.

The words grew in you.
They grew with you each moment
and you carved your poems
until you felt their sinews as your own
giving you a spirit of independence.

In Paris you met Rodin and felt
his sculptures moving upon the air like music,
through the bronze or the stone, supple as the forms of Bernini.

The glorious Salomé danced for you in Russian nights
until your very being sang the praises of trees.

In the shadows of Duino
the luminous angel appeared.

Even in your death you dreamed of beauty,
the cold complex beauty of the universe
unfolding under the wings of your own silent, quivering eyelids.

Rilke in Switzerland

There were nights
when the clouds where domed
as in an El Greco painting,
buoyed as in a giant vessel viewed in the harbour.
Was it in Alexandria or on a balcony in Muzot
you heard the call of the invisible,
the clear resonance of the night owl
swooping down on the dark and craggy slopes
in the lights of stars,
the chandeliers of courtyard parties?

There were moments of your youth
when you touched the earth and the angel.
The door in the sky.
This touching that was all.
Life taught you lessons
and you listened to the patterns
where birth and life begins and you waited.

During the trip to Russia
the words opened up
as you sped through the trees
and you walked with Tolstoy through spring fields.
Lou Andreas would toss her ring
and say you may have it that night.

You remember the women on walks by the sea
and how beautiful they were
standing before the white waves.
Oh, you knew it well,
how they slipped through the sable sands.

The guests are gone.
There are fewer parties this spring.
So this is it.
You come to the threshold of the end,
this mortal coil and the river of blood
moving through the land of your body
a rich tributary—
the song that breaks out of the symphony.
Now death itself is the stranger.
In this distant room among the mountains
you remember your life
as full and buoyant—
and the curve of Lou's cheek.
Life speaks to you
out of this moment of your final flowering
and in its wilting.
The mirror reflects the room
and the separate forms of the things around you.

You reach for an apple.
The air is heavy.
The mirror is now without frame
and the world is you
and the words are now
only a dreaming of wind
and of many rivers running
through your life.

Driving to D.H. Lawrence's Ranch at Saint Cristobal

I

The road is rough.
I pass the tangled cacti,
the twisted shrubs,
the pine cones strewn about the road,
snow at the edge of the field.

The higher we go the wilder it gets.
I am travelling toward the ranch of D.H. Lawrence.
Around Lobo Mountain we move,
leaving the vista behind us.
I can see Lawrence on a horse,
riding from Taos.

II

"The Snake" was the first poem
that I read by Lawrence
under the corrugated roof at Emery.
In the basement bedroom one night
the words awoke me.
I heard a voice I did not recognize as my own
and wrote my first poem.
Now I'm in the mountains of New Mexico
where he wrote the poems
of the Kiowa tribe, the mountain lion and the eagles,
always on his flight to paradise.

The silence extends over the vista
toward the Rio Grande.
Everything is wild,
the woods overgrown
as in an old fairy tale.

D. H. Lawrence sat at the table to write
under the guardian of the tree
that spirals up into the sky.
He saw it as an angel
(Georgia O'Keeffe would paint it).

On the porch
I balance myself on the chair with missing slats
that he made.
I try the knob.
The door to the house is locked.

I peek in,
trying to find my way back
into that time when Lawrence and Frieda
berated each other in the morning
and made love in the small bedroom.

Before me, the wooden desk
he used, and a black typewriter
(where his friend, Bret, typed
"The Woman Who Rode Away,")
the kitchen table,
a photo of D. H. Lawrence.

III

I walk up to the memorial chapel.
Taking out a twig,
I open the door
and see the green laurel leaves.
Over Lawrence's grave,
the phoenix still.

Al Purdy's Place

1

I turn onto the road leading to Ameliasburgh.
Nearly twenty years since
I visited this place where
you wandered under the large beams
through the old grist mill,
searching for dusty motes of sunlight
until you stared into the face of Owen Roblin.

The '73 Ford is gone.
Your tall lanky figure does not stride to meet me again.
The waters of Roblin Lake are rough.
Around broken boards I step
to see blue wooden chairs weathered on the deck.
Eurithe, Michael Ondaatje and Margaret Lawrence
would have drunk beer late into the summer's night.

The old cabin you built as a study is locked.
In the box by the door I see a lamp
that would have shone light
on the hiccoughing typewriter, on the poems
that spoke of Fidel on Revolutionary Square,
of Gus and you before the Kremlin,
searching for the ghost of Helen in the dusty city of Troy,
recounting the tough Tarahumara women in Mexico,
the scenes evoking the ghosts of Machu Picchu and your friend Earl.

You sat in that study until it became the freight car:
across the prairies into the sudden mountains,
until the dust of the land entered
you in those voices,
speaking now through your poems.

You were working on *Reaching for the Beaufort Sea,*
talking about time,
how we continually mourn the past,
how we live on a thin edge,
a slice of time that exists only in the present
before it becomes the past.

2

I remember that letter from Ameliasburgh
that invited me to send you poems.
I still hear your distinct voice,
with its currents of wit and humour,
a gusto, a build-up and release.
I remember the time in El Gitano
after so much sangria
when we argued poetry late into the night.

Through the rough gravel of Purdy Lane,
I drive to the cemetery alongside the river.
There, in the wet grass is the black shiny tome
with the words, "The Voice of the Land."
Someone has left a note
and stuck a ballpoint pen in the earth.

At the Reading of Irving Layton

You emerged with a swagger
into the light of the stage
in jacket and black turtleneck,
your belly bevelled with experience,
your hair beaming silver
radiating its own light.
Your voice was rich full bass
as you savoured the syllables
and the poem leaped from the page,
caught and held us in its attention.

I discovered your poem "The Birth of Tragedy"
in a blue high school poetry anthology,
where you celebrated the poem as a pool
reflecting "Love, power, the huzza of battle."
You showed us what a poet could do
in "A Tall Man Executes a Jig"
when you portrayed artists and philosophers,
their incompleteness on the stage of our lives.

Afterwards I talked to you.
You spoke of what it takes to be a poet,
that it is the role of the poet
to write about this country
with a dynamic, energizing will,
a Dionysian energy.

Your lovers were naked
with desires real as flesh.
Your love in Paris was Aviva,
when you were tapping out poems on her thigh.
Love was the grief for your wild, mad mother.

After the reading I ran
into the crisp autumn night in London.
The moon was never more clear
shining over the rippling austere Thames.

Montreal Troubadour

for Leonard Cohen

1

The ice was almost out of the river
as I drove down the Saint John Valley
with spring in the air.

What was it about your voice
that I heard in your book of poems—
the black book with its gold lettering,
looking like a treasure box?
The room became a microcosm,
the bed become a wafer,
and your Suzanne spoke
of the body of wisdom and the mind.

The vulnerable sensitivity of your soul
created the simplest and most profound scenarios.
For what you did was death defying,
high above on that lonely tightrope of our teenage lives.
When listening to your haunting voice,
we consumed your words like spiritual bread and wine.

2

I arrived at the concert just on time
and took my seat twenty-five feet from the stage.
There you emerged with your fedora and sang,
sang on your knees to the hushed audience
and slowly the arena became a temple.

I learned that you were staying at the Delta Hotel.
In the morning I asked the chambermaid,
"Have you seen Leonard Cohen?"
She looked at me uncomprehendingly.
"No. Does he work here?"

Later at the reception desk I noticed
a man with a beret or an Irish cap
and I realized it was you, Leonard.
I told you the story about the chambermaid.
"That's good ... good," you said,
placing your hand on my shoulder
and we laughed.

Elegy for Louis Dudek

1

It has been snowing on and off all day.
I hear of your death.
Outside the window the wind sweeps across the snow
still as the sea, but the wind gasps.
There is no meaning in its currents.
The world this week seems bleak:
The dictatorships go on and on.
The crows squabble like postmodern critics.

Louis, you believed that poetry could change
something in the world.
This day has a dead silence about it.
There are no flags flying at half-mast.
Your books are not for sale in the malls.

2

You were a maverick.
When you opened your doors at McGill
on Tuesday mornings,
I met Ray Filip with his wry smile,
Marc Plourde, Stephen Morrissey
who had a shy brazen honesty, wrote
"regard as sacred the disorder of my mind."
Ken Norris, who came from New York.

3

As I entered the pillared sanctum
in my Woody Allen lumberjack shirt,
you invited me into your office.

I handed you my orange Killaly Press Chapbook,
"I like that line,
The violet rays of the absolute."

Sometimes I saw you sitting in your captain's chair,
the Polish philosopher who quoted Chinese poets
with that Buddha-like smile.
When you joked
you seemed like an east-end kid.

You published our poetry when no one else would.
In your office made of oak panels as in a ship.
You spoke of poetry as a voyage, as Atlantis,
and we were far from the city for awhile,
deeper into the world to find
the poem beyond the poem.

How you were able to love what words do,
drawing our attention to Michelangelo,
to the way he could create the lines
and bring the sculpture to life out of stone,
to a Beethoven concerto with the notes
almost palpable in the air
tracing the symmetry of music.

The last time we met at your house,
you showed me Sidney's translation of Petrarch,
talked about Mallarmé and chess
and the musical form of Pound and Eliot in the longer poems.
And you said it would be wonderful to be alive
in a hundred years to see what new poetry would bring.
Louis, you leave us in your wake.

4

Outside the world is cold tonight
in this northern New Brunswick city.
Over this white sea,
the wind blows through great crags
and snowflakes are words,
each shaped like so many different lives,
bringing with each thought
something into birth.

Raymond Souster

You were one of the poets who read in a suit
looking like your photo, the banker.
I was drawn to your spare line
and your the immediate voice
evoking the life of Toronto,
the sleepy summer Humber River,
its hidden secrets couched in lush ravines.
Your poems drew subtly
of the desire of lovers
uncovering their shy naked bodies.

You made me recognize the history around me:
the haunting outline of the Old Mill,
sunken vessels off Hanlan's point,
William Lyon Mackenzie rebelling in his Bond Street House.

It was my childhood too—playing cowboys,
sneaking along the stream under sand cliffs,
the farmers chasing us from apple orchards,
the surreal ride on the Sunnyside roller coaster,
penny arcades, peep shows, Siamese twins in a bottle.

You captured the moments in still life:
a newsstand man hawking his papers in summer heat,
an Aboriginal woman fighting off drunken men
(I saw them in the bars on Gerrard Street),
the boys shining shoes under palace cinema lights,
the armless war veterans with their medals.
We could not walk past them.

No one has painted this city as you have.

Drinking with John Newlove in the Westbury Hotel

In the Westbury Hotel we sit at the bar
sipping the stories
between the beer and the silence.
A waiter keeps serving us drinks
while around us the world grows green
as a jungle or a giant aquarium.

You speak of how hard
it is to live fighting the bottle,
to find the truths
and to keep them.

Sitting at the edge of the bar
in the darkness of Conrad's night
you breathe with emotion,
words bitten in the mouth,
cool on the tongue
as we speak of the walls of existence
which sometimes remains like pieces of a poem
we do not want to write.

The luau girl folds the serviettes on tables
as music hovers around our heads
like the blue smoke of your cigarette
and Madonna's voice breaks
down in the wild stillness.
We hold the cold bevelled glasses closer.

Ammonite

You sit on the antique table,
coiled in your mollusc shape.
Millions of years ago
you swam in the Pacific Ocean
shaped by the water
and later forged by fire until
you become a jewel—
a gyre that we follow in our own path.

You fly toward the surface where you feed.
So we too move in night's dream
diving through timeless seas
or leaping beyond the edge of our daily lives
mapping out a new direction.

You are an ancient ammonite named after a ram's horn
of the Egyptian God of procreation.
I see the molecular design for your different roles.
Now you are a talisman
revealing the secret rings of your travel
in the houses of the constellations:
Aries, Cancer, Scorpio, Aquarius.
They are suspended in the silver-blue nebulae.
And inside the capsules
—of egg or pear—
the x-ray of an embryo
floating in the amniotic fluid.

You are a mandala, ancient mollusc
revealed in your shapes, colours, textures
a mosaic of the universe
inscribed in the holy scroll of your body.

The Last Visit to My Father

Would you recognize me?
It has been months since I've seen you.
You don't look directly at me.
When I ask you,
"Who am I?"
you look distracted,
reach into your thoughts
but can't come up with an answer.
"I haven't a clue ... Herman?"

I show you my book.
"When did you write that?"
a flicker of recognition in your eyes,
then your attention leaves.
My sister, Ellie, tries to prod your memory
with big band era songs and family photos,
but you seem locked in your private space,
uttering phrases that are hard to hear,
that only have significance to you.

In the sunset room you look at the old home movies
of the five brothers' reunion in Donegal.
Your attention is drawn to scenes you have filmed:
the grey house, the haggard cliffs,
the long brown beaches.
These are distantly familiar to you
in a life that once was your Ireland.

You try to put it into some whole
piece by fractured piece
but your words are lost
in the crash of the surf and
the jangled currents of your memory.

Just before our imminent departure,
and perhaps sensing our leaving,
you suddenly turn to me
for the first time in the afternoon,
look deeply into my eyes, and say,
"Is that you Laurence?"

Herman

That first sunny morning at Katwijk
we climbed the white-ribbed sand
of the dunes and waving grass
and the water sparkled blue and gold.

When I was seven I crossed
the hallway to your bedroom;
you sat by the window, painting.
It took you weeks to shape your Canadian mountains
stroke by stroke.
You formed the forest,
the grey-purple glaciers,
a white peak shining in a windy sky.

Smoking in your room you described
the war, how you dragged firewood
through heavy snow avoiding the patrol.
Outside the Hague you gave an orange
to a starving old man.

We drove to Jasper in the mountains,
sailed across the blue, crystal lake
on a wooden raft like Jim and Huckleberry Finn.
Later, heading east,
you drove the prairies in a day
down the Lakehead past Nipigon.
We laughed and told legends of the Aboriginals.
The moon was a red volcano.

At Horseshoe, we skied down the mountainside
over the high banked edges
                    and the curving moguls
down through the slopes
                            of that white and silver sea

down through the silence into evenings
                    around our stove and coffee.

I see you now
no other way than in motion:
sailing across Georgian Bay
skating down the Humber River
skiing down the mountainside.

You refused me nothing Herman:
uncle, brother, painter, clown, hero,
as generous as the colours
and forms of the earth.

Unfinished Portrait

for Roberta

1

We drive under a clear November sky.
The road winds out along the hills,
follows the river line
past the streams
that flow through the matted golden reeds,
and the land sweeps out toward the Petitcodiac.

You are happy this afternoon,
moving your whole body to the long rifts
of The Doors' "Light My Fire."
The landscape rises, twists, turns.
"This is what I live to see."

The land has a clarity.
The last silver poplar leaves
still flicker in the sun.
We are driving toward Moncton
feeling the music.

2

Now is twilight.
I sit on the side of the bed
looking at paintings
taken out of your portfolio of uncollected works:
the painting of a woman in a red dress
ensconced in a shell
and the blue one you were wearing.
The landscape of your house in Midway
with exotic red lights on trees
has a hint of Monet.

As my eyes strain, I see
the portraits of your old boyfriends:
the truck driver already dead,
the idealized one who did prison time,
the intellectual who warned us
about your erratic behaviour.

There is a portrait of Father
recalling old photos of Errol Flynn,
a portrait of a mermaid,
with a luminous green tail and
a Marilyn Monroe smile.
(That time in Montreal you were
so alive the city around you with your
blond flowing hair, infectious smile,
and memorable wit.)

I remember your breakdown when
you spent six weeks confined in
Ravenscrag on the mountain in Montreal.
Your paintings grew
past your schizophrenia.

This room now becomes a gallery
of the scenes of your life
in this early evening.

We Find Each Other Before the Waterfall

The place is so peaceful.
The two trees are reflected in the pond.
I can see them clearly.

I say, "Show yourself to me."
"I will show you myself," you say.
You look into my eyes
and you do show me yourself.

Your eyes are green pools.
I see myself in your eyes.

There is a movement,
the slow movement of horses.
Your eyes have a naked beauty.

I'm alive to all around me.
The pond becomes your painting.
I see the concealed blues,
the far reds,
the edge of ferns.

I hear the voice of the waterfall
as your inner voice.
In the centre of the pond
the pagoda is our temple.
You and I reflected in the water,
are those two trees.

You

I hear you softly climb the stairs
in this stillness before the thunderstorm.
Suddenly you appear before me in the room.
My eyes take in your nakedness
as you slip into the sheets.
How do you have this power to wake me?
It makes me move against your whole body.
The kiss and the motion of your tongue
are speaking desire
they are moving on me
I'm moving on you
I taste your body
you laugh like a brook.
Eva: I say your name.
I forget your name.
Then it is reborn
in the parts of your body.
I'm learning a new language
The words become a song.
Kiss me back into life,
let me feel the subtle rhythm of your tides.
Day disappears into night.
I'm one with you.

Your Painting

for Eva

How is it that you are able to paint light
and ask us to reconsider what light is?
Or rain.
The spectrum of the rain
that is breaking up
into unrecognizable shapes of the city
in the fractured neon bursts.
It seems the light is raining
or is it raining light?
And we pause to listen to rain
in the continual jazzy night.
How do you break up the wetness of air,
its silvery sheen lines,
into the explosive red traffic lights
or the yellow sceptre of lamps?

How do you paint water's ebb and flow,
as if it were you looking at the water
until it becomes part of you?

When you paint the landscape
you draw us into a pale meditative sky.

Musée Rodin

The stone does not die,
but lives on against the green of this garden.

Outside sun rays
palpitate on passing tourists.

Here among *Le Cathedral*,
La Main de Dieu, *Adam et Eve*,
people talk about the stone sculptures.

Do they not breathe
a different air?

The white stones move
against the cameras;
the chandeliers shimmer,
colour marble pieces
evoke the sea.

Time does not touch the stone.
Miss Eve Fairfax:
breathe.

World is rearranged
by sharp, striking forms.

Water rises from
a fresh fountain.

Moving in the mind,
a continuous wind.

Wheat Field with Crows

after Van Gogh

The painting sings.
It is crazy with life
with all the crows gathering
over the wheat field.
The wheat is moving
with the wind
moving in the wings
of the crows
moving in the waves
in the surge
of the feelings
moving with desire
beyond itself.
The crows cawing,
thronging in the open sky.

Crow

You, black morning bird,
wake me out of dream
in your raw hunger,
in your appetite
for carrion.
No roosters in these city streets,
only you, crow
reeling through the luminous avenues of sky
in the cawing voice.
Something in me wants that,
that caw, that cacophony,
that rough gravelled sound.
You are my shadow.
Speak out of the shadow.
Your voice is the voice of the grey country sky
coming out of the dawn.
Black ministering bird,
I see you wheeling above the pines,
I see you perched on the burnt branches
at the edge of the golf course and the teeming swamp.
On my journeys you are at the roadside
with your beak tearing the meat,
cleaning the white bones of death.
Your flight is wild in my dreams.

Iris

after Van Gogh

This flower in its various shades
of purple and blue,
wrapped in its gauze casing,
has just come out of its cocoon.
The colours meld,
blues changing in a late twilight.
It is the iris of the eye
altering the optic perspective,
the membrane before the mind.

Look at this flower,
the way the calyx holds the petals,
the wild tapered leaves reaching
their tentacles toward the light.

Van Gogh has painted them
as if they were thrust out of the ground.
The flower is the centre,
but everything grows outward,
the blades of the grass rising
(don't forget the ghostly mauve and blue irises yet to bloom)
and the yellow flowers
gathered in twos, threes and fours
like kids in a schoolyard.
The more light you let in,
the more you see.

The grass blowing,
the iris growing out of its background
opening into its own blue being.

Two Pink Shells

after Georgia O'Keeffe

The light falls onto the shells,
along the grooves,
a spectrum of pink, purple, mauve.

It shines into the centre of the shell,
a white glove,
a vessel to catch the rays.

The two shells
placed one beside the other.

They are so comfortable
in the rough texture of the lines
of their rising curves.

The shell is not a container,
but a form of birth
opening out into the world.

Kakabeka Falls, Kaministiquia River

after Lucius R. O'Brien

This painting is about sound,
the kinaesthetic intermingling of the water,
the vegetation with foliage so rich and red
struggling with the cold.
Water flows to the edge
of canvas, spills out into
the bubbling of
the corner, sending
sound, colour, light
everywhere.
You can hear the water
in the white luminous paint;
see the colours transform sound.
Follow the river into the falls—
over the shiny, polished rocks
into the foreground of the canvas.
See how the whiteness swirls into the foam,
over the billion-year-old rocks
below their totem forms.

Zest

The white bitter pulp
makes the taste buds stand up:
feel the split, the crackle, the dazzle.
Feel the spray, a sea-wave
around the coastal edges.
Let your lips be the beach,
roll the soft tongue into the grooves
of the orange.
This is the way to taste your life,
a heaven-blessed inlet,
a droplet of perfume,
the perfect quenching of thirst,
that satisfaction—
what your mouth was born to do.

The Dance of Margie Gillis

I see you moving tensely on the stage
out of darkness toward the light
with subtle movements
as you become the motion of music:
arms, elbows, shoulders, thighs
bend and swirl into the branches of trees and wind.
How you live in the body of music.

You dance the pain of women
alone in farmhouse kitchens,
of women in the labour of childbirth,
With the scarlet ribbon around you
you carve the words of freedom.

Dream the dance, dance the dream.
This is the soul's choreography,
this is the clear passion of geometry,
the lexicon of love.

Dance through the stages of life.
As you struggle, we struggle
in this fulcrum of life and death,
trying to see the heavens
beyond the breathing of our fatigued bodies.

Dance until our bodies move us
into the central light of the finale,
the exulting glow of departure
in the dance   the dance

"The seal's wide spindrift gaze toward paradise" *

for Robert Bly

The fishing boat pulls out into the harbour,
past the mammoth hulk of a bow,
which rears its scaly dragon carcass out of the water.
Once a five-masted schooner,
used as a casino and bordello in Boston,
now it's a vast nest for cormorants.

This afternoon we ride the water,
the wake spreading out behind us.
Roots are like the large twisted limbs
of serpents and chimeras growing through
the shale tablets of the earth,
floating by like an ancient diorama.

Out of the shore the albino tree stands
with not a single leaf on its bleached branches,
destroyed by the guano of the osprey,
who sits perched on the throne of twigs.
Someone calls out, "eagle's nest,"
and Humberto draws his finger after the eagle.
We speak about the love poems of Neruda,
the kingly bird circling above the trees.

Humberto, your face is strong and radiant
as a Mayan mask,
expressing the hidden emotion,
the shapes and colours of your language.

---

* Hart Crane

I ask you to write the words
of the mouth of the river,
Ri vchi ri limi.
The words turn the water blue.
The sun radiates over the waves,
the birds flying over the patina of the speeding boat.
I want to see the seals.

Suddenly they are there in their miraculous presence,
sunbathers with their aureoled heads in water.
You can see myth there.
They are like their Donegal cousins,
taking on the shape of the women,
splash through the foamy water,
disappear into a dive and then reappear.
Beyond them the pines wave
like giant prehistoric fronds in the wind.
"The seal's wide spindrift gaze toward paradise."

Café Terrace at Night

after Van Gogh

Such a great painting—
you feel you could just walk
onto those cobblestones,
hear your feet echo through
the lighted streets.

It's such a great painting,
that contrast between
the gold lights of the café,
and the blueness of the night sky.

You feel you could walk in—
sit down at one of those white marble tables
(how symmetrical they are).

You could walk into this painting
and listen to the late night gossip, hear
the people talking about love, work,
little things that make up their lives.

You could walk into those streets,
passing the houses with their dark
human secrets looking down.

You could walk in, order a drink,
have a seat, contemplate.
The passing drama of life is here
floating in the bright parasols of midnight.

Poetry Reading Dream

Have you ever been in a dream
and tried to read the poem you wrote
or at least imagined you wrote
but couldn't because it isn't there?
I'm going through the pages
but the book is nearly blank.
There is not one single fully recognizable poem.
This is a nightmare.

I continue going through the books
and now I'm starting to lose it.
Every time I find a book
there is something wrong with it
and the audience is getting larger,
people hanging all over the place.
I scavenge through the archival pile
looking for the poetry in all this mess.

Suddenly something wonderful happens
and the small dingy fake Parisian studio space
becomes a large Montreal *bibliothèque.*
Half the walls disappear.
I'm in a country world with parks and rivers and mountains
and I feel as high as a mountain and begin with a poem.

I was walking in the city,
and there was music everywhere
and everything was light, light.
There was a rhythm
in every motion, every thought, every glance
and I was enjoying it, grooving with it.
My body's swinging and moving.

You have to look for the mountains in the city.
You didn't know that they have mountains in Montreal.
Look at them ladies and gentlemen.
Look beyond your library eyes to the glowing peaks.
Feel the mountains in your blood, in your hands, in your feet.
Let them sing in your veins.
Let them tell you how to speak.
Let them swing, shake and break you.
Let the mountains speak within you
from every corner of your life,
from every lighted space of your being.
Let them sing,
out of every neglected moment,
out of every impossible dream.
Let the mountains sing with you.
Let them awaken you to their eyes.
And the audience is swaying.
They are with me.
I can see the city-mountains in their eyes.
I can feel the excitement in their veins.
I can sense the hunger for the ordinary.
I can touch their elemental game.
Why can't every reading be like this?

In Mondrian's Whirlpool

I slip into another world
as bubbles burst around.
My fingers explore the marble map
of Mondrian's tableaux,
probe dendritic streams.
Through the dark Saint Lawrence I drift
back to the green, violent Tiber
out into the glassy imperial Nile,
back to a nameless river
that winds between steamy Palaeozoic hills.
The moon cruises through a sensual haze.
Here the words rise up like warriors
and Max Ernst's purple mastodons roam.
Matisse's couples amorously play
and the waves break on the Happy Isles.
And I float freely
through a dream
among pastel forms
in Mondrian's whirlpool.

The Poet

for Rolf Harvey

Swinging your trumpet from side to side
you strode down Habitant Drive singing,
"For young Roddy McCorley goes to die
On the bridge of Toome today."
You made yourself out of that struggle,
typing in the dungeon late into the night.
There you would sit by the redwood desk
under the painting of cabin in the Swiss Alps
with the old Royal typewriter with uneven keys
gleaming like an old altar
to write poems of invective and satire,
metaphors darkly etched on onionskin paper.
You chronicled the pain of your mother,
your father, a handsome moustached gentleman in his sports coat
who played jazz in the big band in the thirties on the circuit,
working now in the block house of Vicks VapoRub.
We read Cohen and listened to the raspy voice of Dylan
on the Seabreeze Record Player,
or Rachmaninoff's "Rhapsody on a Theme of Paganini,"
the harsh beats evoking
the violinist's triumphant struggle with the devil
and the music rose before the dungeon's dark curtains.
We scribbled signatures—
Karl Wolf, Mark Thorpe, John McCue—on furnace pipes.
And I would walk home
in my own snow soliloquies
with the wind whirling stories in their own currents,
watching my shadow
grow longer in arched haloed light,
having before me the dark citadel of Emery
beyond the pines.

The Artist Surveys His Broken Glass Sculptures

I was standing in the courtyard
with the artist talking about his sculptures:
tall wave fronds,
sea urchins or barnacles.
Suddenly the wind changed,
leaves tossed in a turbulence of air.

The colour of the sky and lake grew darker
and the artists' tents began blowing open like sails,
paintings flew from their moorings
and the rain started.

Through the arch of the pavilion
out on Lake Ontario over the breakwater
the waves were crashing.

The glass artist stood musing.
His face was shining in the rain.
He collected what was left on the floor
gathered them up like broken decanter tops
or shattered ice cubes.

He looked around relieved:
his crystal fish still intact,
the large iconic glass forms in their own personal myth
still standing against the shore of the lake.
He smiled knowing that he had survived this storm
and in this act of resilience
he impressed me more than anything.

The Almond Blossoms

after Van Gogh

As diverse as life,
the branches move only
the way branches do,
pale white petals open,
almost birds in flight.

I'm in Herman's studio.
He is painting the windmill,
the fields of tulips along the canals.
Beyond the white screen
of his canvas
the wide blue sky.

It is spring.
The blossoms thick
as curtains.

The windmill
is turning.
I'm in the windmill.

November Blues

Then glut thy sorrow on a morning rose,
Or on the rainbow of the salt sand-wave
      —John Keats

November, dark short month so long
half season between the holiday of remembrance
and that of a holy birth.
I waken with sad circular thoughts
that do not reach beyond themselves.

There is no clear waking, but a pervasive mist
that shrouds my early morning rituals—
not the warm Brazilian coffee
(its image of lighted leaves in the rainforest)
not the aromatic raisin and cinnamon bagels,
nor the friendly smiling Quaker with his hearty oats.
No, these don't make me feel better.

But mood can change like the sharp autumnal weather,
for nothing can foresee what changes will take place.
So, is that not always the challenge—
to find the joy in darkness
as Keats found it in his flight to the nightingale?
Light is the other side of darkness on this coin.
In the lines of poetry the poet becomes nature.
Then art, and its reflection of our mortal state,
reveals its power and transforming energy.

It is here at the end of an afternoon
that I see the sun for the first time today,
making a corona of the clouds,
showing all the tones of whites and greys.
If I could capture that scene in my painting
it would be the light I need.

Now, when I look toward the bright evening sky,
I see these dark dreams are only a part of the whole.
I remember the old books in my pine bookcase,
and how the songs of rock 'n' roll revived me,
Beethoven's Symphony No. 7
Miles Davis' extemporaneous notes in this blue November.

Winter Scene

after Li Po

Dark when I awake.
I move across cool linoleum.
The kitchen bright, but morning far.
There must be a full moon.
Mist drifts across the river,
veiling silver trees.
When I raise my eyes to sky I expect
the silver cup of the moon,
but sky is empty.
Where is the light coming from?
I look down to bright mirror,
iridescent blanket, first snow.

Two Maps of Emery
(2016)

Toronto Maple Leaf Stadium

We got off the clanging streetcars
moved among the throngs of people,
vendors hawking baseball programs
pennants, bats and other souvenirs.
We followed the ramp
that spiralled among the peeling stucco walls
with vaulted windows swooped by vagrant pigeons,
and emerged into the early evening air,
the players already warming up on the infield
throwing their deadly accurate baseballs.

I was twelve years old, with the other Sunday School boys.
Mr. Upton puffed his cigar, exhaled purple smoke,
spoke of the strategies as if he were the coach.
There was always something happening out there
before the islands on the lake
when the freighter's foghorn bellowed through the night,
and the mysterious aroma from the malt silos
permeated the dusky air.
A biplane trailed the cryptic messages
of unknown lovers across the mauve curtain of the sky,
and men in candy striped suits barked out orders,
threw bags of peanuts across rows of unruly fans.

It was hard to focus our attention
until the sun faded under the blue bars of evening,
dissolving into the night and the lights flashed on.
The outfield became greener,
and light more intense on the infield.

The action drew us into
the secret codes of pitchers and catchers.
The loud judgment of umpires called players out,
to the protests of coaches.

Then the player drove the ball
through the gap
and the crowd rose to the edge of its seats.
Through memory's lens
we don't remember when or
who turned the play of the game.
Maybe it was one of the best sluggers, Steve Demeter,
sliding into a kind of dusty glory
to that safe plate at home
in the diamond light of the stadium by Lake Ontario.

Miss Christopherson's Writing Club

She sat on the corner of the desk
wearing a tight black dress
with her long legs in black stockings
and her hair tumbled like that of a movie star.
In grade eight extracurricular activities,
I gave up basketball and volleyball
to join the school newspaper.
When she asked me to find a story,
I interviewed the players
after our victory on the ice.
As she read my writing,
I looked at the freckles around her neck
and just above her breasts
while perfume wafted over me
like a tropical breeze.
She drove us into a kind of frenzy,
like a woman from playboy foldouts.
Was there anything more powerful
than a thirteen-year-old's fantasy of Miss Christopherson?

The Red Nib Pen

It was a modern version of the quill,
in that tradition of Shakespeare and Dickens
or the art of Chinese ideograms.
In autumnal season of grade eight,
attaching the nib to the pen,
I tried to master the art of penmanship,
the loops of the " *f* " or "*l*" or the curve of "*a*" or "*r*"
the symmetrical "*k*" or the eccentric "*q*"
making the sound of a skater on hard ice,
grooving the letters onto the blue lines of the foolscap.

I copied Bliss Carman's, "A Vagabond Song"
the formal treaty articles of England and America
that ended the War of 1812,
Thomas Edison's inventions,
the story of intergalactic space travel.

Then one day we put away the pens.
They were gone like the scarlet CN trains
or the passenger ships on the Great Lakes.
The next year in high school
in the factory-like typing class
the Underwood typewriters clanged
their bells at the end of every line.

Sportsland Park

T. Alec Rigby, a deep-sea diver and lumberjack
in the early 1960s, created Sportsland Park,
the largest swimming pool in the world—
so large it had to be patrolled by lifeguards on horseback.

Because Rigby had owned a concrete company
he could afford to put all that cement into
a swimming pool about the size of ten pools.
Each year brought new attractions:
the arcade where you could practice shooting a rifle,
the pinballs machines which lit up and clanged.
Trampolines were built into the ground
and there was a golf range and a stable to rent horses.

There were the days when the CHUM 1050 crew
broadcast from the trampoline area,
and Bob McAdorey tossed out 45s
into a crowd of stampeding teenagers.

My friend, Karl knew a way to sneak in by the back,
hide our bikes under the trees,
then slip through the barbed wire fence.

On the last day of the season I tried the high board.
With an autumn chill in the air
I swam out to the tower, climbed
the white steel rungs to the top board.
Looking down, I could see the farmland to the north,
the cars streaming along the 400.
The great pool stretched before me.
I walked out to the end of the board
and jumped out,
with that great feeling
of momentary suspension,

that delicious falling through the air
down into the depths,
surfacing through the bubbles into the fresh sunlight.
The season was over.

Next year the pool was closed.
An aquamarine shell looked like ruined baths of Caracalla,
the water seeping slowly through its cracked surfaces.

Riding the Night Freight Train
from Jasper to Edmonton

Waiting for the 404 express,
we listen to rumbling of freight cars
on the last night of our trip.
It is time to jump
and we scramble with our bags,
running alongside the train,
looking for an open car,
but there was none.
We could only reach the oil platform.

We are moving away
from the chalet on The Whistlers,
the twinkling lights of Cottonwood Campground
(where we carved our names in the pine beams)
passing by the churning Athabasca River,
and the road out to Maligne Canyon.

We hold onto the side bar
when the long curving train
is accelerating into the mountains
with high cliffs.
Leaning against the railing
like a banister before a huge theatre, we sing
"It's been a hard day's night,
I should be sleeping like a log."

The mountain swallows us
and we hold onto the oil dome
as the train winds in a serpentine motion,
past mountain peaks like ancient tyrants,
violent rivers, silver eskers
under the bronze helmet of the moon.

Beyond the mountains,
through the acrid smell of lumber,
the train stops at the mill town.
The guard patrols the platform
as we huddle against the black dome.
His search light passes over us.

As the train accelerates through the darkness
gliding in its sublunary flight
I try to keep awake.
The night becomes primeval,
creatures breathing in thick swamps,
the green light surreal
as I dream of crashing
into the hidden depths of the lake.

Under a pale Martian sky
the train slows down,
passing grain elevators and spectral towers,
reaching the outskirts of the city.
It's time to jump.
A CN cop sees us
and with rolled up sleeping bags
we begin running
into the rays of the rising sun.

Writing

One night I heard the words,
I could see them on the page,
and I understood what they meant.
The words brought the side of me which was hidden.

Outside, I walked down into the snowy ravine
and emerged into a field of light, the sky
with the red ribbed sand bars was like the sea
and I felt that I could bring to life
everything with words.

My father brought home an old Royal typewriter
from the 1920s with its high front like a forehead,
black as a Model T car with the revolving ribbon
the letters on the keys encased in silver rings
and I would punch them with my fingers
impressing meanings onto the textured page.

The Deserted TTC Tram

On a cold February afternoon Les and I trudged through
the snow up the old farmer's road in Emery.
We saw the tram in the distance, so strange
in this farm setting, like an old sailing vessel
anchored on the sea while the wind blew
the spray of the snow across its dark face.

Through an open window we crawled inside.
The cold wind whistled in broken window panes.
The seats were replaced by shelves with boxes.
We opened one after another,
held the decals in our fingers:
hockey players, football quarterbacks,
Royal Canadian Mounties, rodeo cowboys on horses.
We stuffed quickly them into our pockets
then decided to take the boxes and left
through the darkening landscape.

In the springtime, a policeman arrived at our house.
"Someone has reported that you have decals on your bike.
Where did you get them from?"
My father stood with his arms crossed in the doorway.
The week before he had papered the spare room with them.

Now, thirty-three years later,
I ask Evelyn Thomas about Mr. Storer,
"Do you remember the tram?"
"Yes, he kept merchandise there."
"We stole some of those decals."
"It doesn't matter now," she said,
"The street car burned down a long time ago.
Walt Disney has the copyright."

400 Drive-In

Beyond the farmer's field just below Highway 7
rose the giant slanted screen where Father
would takes us in the 58 Pontiac,
up old Weston Road to the 400 Drive In.
The block letters of the double feature lit up
and my sisters in their pyjamas
would run up to the playground
to swing and slide under the giant dancing
hotdogs and animated Coca-Cola cups
until the first movie began.

From the slightly raised banks we watched
the family movies: *The Big Circus,*
the tightrope walker crosses Niagara Falls,
Jason and the Argonauts—
the heroes battling the skeletons.
The war film: *The Bridge on the River Kwai.*

One night with Johnny Wolf we decided to sneak in,
we crawled through the woods past the lines of cars,
the pay booth, and suddenly the guard
with a flashlight appeared,
"What the hell are you guys doing here?"
We began to run through the slippery gravel,
past the cars with the teenage lovers
entwined before steamy dashboards,
past the surprised older couples who looked at us
out beyond the lighted barge of the snack bar.

The guard chased us
and we were running like soldiers
through a minefield in war films
until the screen grew smaller, diminishing into the sky.

Then were alone in the swamps with the frogs croaking,
the crickets humming,
the bulrushes and the yellow flowers drooping,
the night cool and misty around us
and the cars driving up the 400 like aliens.

Here I am again:
the farms and the forest gone,
the gigantic star ship Cineplex Theatre
has replaced the drive-in.
I walk right past the gate
with no attendant about to chase me.
I sit and watch the huge screen with the constellations
like that night long ago,
listening to the music of *Star Wars*
and the rolling of the credits.

On the way out I meet Helen
with thin grey hair and wavering eyes,
"Yes, I've been here since the theatre opened."
"Did you ever go to the 400 Drive-In?"
"Yes, We drove up from the city with my family."
"Do you remember what movies you saw?"
"Nah, I can hardly remember yesterday."

Return to Emery

1

The traffic is busy
when we drive to the Crang's estate.
Across the road was a ranch style house
with a bomb shelter.
Behind in the forest of trilliums I found antlers.
In the closest house to Crang's estate
my friend, John Bradley, lived.
One warm autumn day
we crept by the hedge to view
the swimming pool, a place of wild parties.

We traced our steps to the orchard,
climbed up into the trees,
eating large yellow apples
when a man in a plaid jacket called out.
"Enjoying the apples boys?
Come on down now.
Run along and take some apples with you."
It was Mr. Crang.

Now the door opens again
and I recognize the priest
from my previous visit with Tim Lambrinos.
In his living room
he speaks of the history of the house
built as a summer home by Percy Gardiner
who made a fortune in metals in the '30s
Over the door the sign in Latin:
Unfortunate those who arrive and no one is home.

I ask if we can view Crang's Pond.
He leads us into a priest's room
with empty bookshelves
"No one reads books anymore
it's a different world ... digital."
He opens the curtains,
the spring light over the pond
illuminated it as an icon.

Slowly we cross the football field,
trying to find a way to Crang's Pond,
but tangled branches and dead trunks
along the shore prevents us from entering
until we find a gap.
The pond is smaller than it was
when formed in the 1950s.

Here below the Tudor mansion
we played hockey games after school.
Sometimes after a game I would put my Sherwood
down and skate across the glittering ice
over the dark underwater with sleeping reptiles,
the wild gold braids of weeds
like those of mythical girls ...

2

There is one last place that I want to show Eva.
Across from the hill at Emery Collegiate
was the large forest of jack pine, white pine, spruce
that extended from Coronado Court
half a mile to Habitant Drive.
There before the high ridge, the Emery Creek
would have carved its course for thousands of years,
undulating back and forth, past high cliffs of sand,
gathering at places into ponds.

This is the place where I saw
the hawk glide and encountered a fox,
the artesian well in the log cabin,
a bridge above the trilobites in the bank.
I named this place my Robinson Crusoe Island.
Now it is construction site
with oversized bulldozers.
The earth is hardened clay
like an old Roman highway,
broken rock, gravel, muddy water.
What happened to the pine trees?

On the hillside the shrubs
tossed and turned
like the aftermath of a flood—
even the shape of the hills has changed.
The stream is now caged in a net of rocks
and the water does not have that old music.

I'm looking for something ...
and when I see large spreading willow
I know where I am.
Between the trees
no longer a road but a path,
is a long green carpet of grass
reaching to the top of the hill—
the old farmer's road.
This is where our trips began,
where we climbed to the top
to see the old abandoned Usher barn
where we heard
Johnny Wolf telling us about the decals.
This road led to the Storer's tram.
This was the land of Isaac Devins.

I call Eva to come
and standing on the ridge of the hill
I could see the larger lines of the land,
Emery Collegiate on the summit
where the farm with the old trunks was,
the large pines before Habitant Arena.
This is the place I remember, my place
where the Humber River flows.

The House of Shifting Time
(2019)

Travel

When I walked into the timeless night
and felt the twilight's mauve air changing,
when my flashlight became
a beacon to scan the stars,
I would direct my path
above the garden's green genius,
up to the trees whose large leaves turned fluorescent,
and farther, outward, beyond the clouds.
The child in me still shines in the cavern's moment.

Night Express to the Maritimes

for Al Moritz

Through city streets the bus launches
into the storm. Already the terrain
outside is unfriendly,
the air monsoon wild.
People peer into night's mirror,
move restlessly on worn upholstery.

A young woman clasps her cell phone
as her lover's words break into static,
her voice rising,
"You better not have a girl in our bedroom!"

A man looks out into the night,
remembers his friend bleeding on the cobblestones,
pile of pills spilled around him,
sirens following the night,
crazy candy—coloured cop car lights
fracturing the air,
breaking through mist.

The Filipino woman beside me
grasping the seat as if it were a reef
speaks about visiting her husband.
Who are you?
Are you my mother?

A young couple smile,
tell how they rode the weekend's high
wave after wave of desire.

Slowly the rain trickles, ebbs, stops. A mist
hangs on the highway's shoulders,
on large trees gathered together.
The grey sky is still, waiting for dawn.

Cloud Watching at Night

On the midnight express to Montreal, I gaze at rocky beaches, ruined docks, village lights. And the clouds. As I travel they change forms, illuminated by the moonlight. They are shamans, transforming themselves from seal to whale—those forms Hamlet pointed out to Polonius over Elsinore's dark parapets.

By the long reach of Saint Lawrence River, the clouds are drifting on the night's silver screen, emerging as coasts and mountains. Influenced by water, currents and fire flow, the blue and grey outlines of elements continue their evolution.

I'm reading the clouds now, their shapes are the primordial words of the world.

The Blue Canoe

for Gerry Kemp

It is difficult to get to the river,
the road tracks rough and moist after winter.
We finally canoe through the bog;
the water has never been so high,
the ordinary boundaries are gone.

Under the twisted white pine trunk
a pheasant had curled into a death fall,
hurling from the storm, broke its neck
on the ice.

Canoeing through the forest
among the bushes,
we slowly start to feel the paddle's rhythm
in a current moving to the river.

In a slender illusion of birches
I see the phantom canoe
with one good paddle on the gunnel
attached by a blue cord,
like a strange omen
anchored by its absent owner.

Follow the River

The land is awakening.
The river is winding between the ridges.
As I drive off the highway
through the brown ribbed mud
and the Moses bulrushes,
I see a sign: Antiques and Old Books.
A dog uncurls from his morning nap,
a man steps out into a patch of sunlight.

Inside, from a glass cabinet
he takes out a book written by Colonel Baird,
with a map of names,
speaking about the history of this land.
The black river coils on the page like a child's drawing.

I feel the presence
of settlers erecting the shell of this house,
the horses hauling the timber through the snow.
I can see the colonel
turning on the coal oil lamp to write
how they came to be
here in New Brunswick in the first place.

This book becomes a gate,
open to the sounds of this place,
flying over the hypnotic flow of the river.

Variations on the River, Fredericton

Saturday morning begins with the news:
bombing of a nightclub in upscale Bogota,
a polygamist in Utah sentenced for having five wives.
The street lamps are fading.
In the market a man carries meat carcasses,
an old woman displays her *croissants aux amandes*.
My daughter Emma arranges
her collection of jewellery on the stand.

In the car, I turn the radio on.
The familiar rhythm of the music
and the windshield wipers are in sync.
The road is leading me out of the city
under the railway stone arches.
Strands of music turn, recede
in harmony with the curves of the road.
I can now read the score of river,
its deeper, darker movements,
the secret of the stream
running through the marsh.
I recall hearing *Folk Song Suite* by Vaughan Williams.
Why is that it I have never noticed
the power of blossoms—their own music
or the white pine smudged against the sky,
the spring following the variations of the river?

Antiques in Spring Light

The sunshine is radiant in the kitchen,
on the lines and curves of chairs.
The blue and gold tablecloth
is textured like a Vermeer painting.

On the table are a variety of oranges,
the fuzzy kiwi,
the bananas in the basket.

I see myself on shelves seasoned by books,
in the old barn door that became a table,
in the icebox with its streaks of sea blue paint.

Last summer I stripped it down
until the grain appeared
with the crosscuts on the surface,
the texture of my skin.

I applied the beeswax,
through the cracks
until the wood healed itself.

Against the green wall the hutch stands—
how pale it was at first,
but slowly over time
it ripened into an amber.
Now the light reflects from it,
filling the whole living room.

King's County Jail

After the hot blinding sun, we enter the cool dark cells,
turned into the exhibition rooms
prominently displaying the province's history—
luxurious ships on the Saint John River,
extravagant parties on decks lasting deep into the night.

I see a baby doll in a pioneer crib.
In the corner, "Grey Ghost," a rocking horse
constructed out of newspaper.
I hear the laughter of children swimming in the creek.

Arranged on a table are manuals
for young ladies and gentlemen.
Cicero's rhetoric, Masefield's renowned sea poems,
novels showing courageous boys tackling the wilderness,
music, poetry and embroidery studies.

In contrast to this is the photograph—
a studio shot of the battlefield.
Machine guns at the soldiers' feet,
each soldier with a sly smile.
Their war had not yet begun;
they don't know the carnage that will face them
at Somme, Vimy Ridge, and Passchendaele.

At the corridor's end I draw a heavy door back.
In a darkroom with discordant images
two mannequins with broken parts sealed with scotch tape
are lying on the floor
near an old rifle and a bear trap.
A doll looks at me with forlorn eyes.

The Anaesthetist's Wife

I am now Princess Anaesthesia.
Ingrid Bergman's face of a vanished Russian line.
The coldness encloses me. Will you let
me out of this anaesthetist's dream,
where my soul hibernates?
I become Sleeping Beauty in the Lake District,
or an ever-lost Fräulein weeping in the Rhineland.
Glacier mirrors reflect our aging faces.

Walking Through Odell Park
on a Rainy Sunday Morning

for Brian Bartlett

I come to the crossways of paths.
Which one to take?
As I climb up the hill,
misty rain falls,
glows on amber woodchips.
I hear the raven's throaty caw.

Balsam is used for Christmas trees,
               basswood for turnery and pianos,
butternut for cabinets,
       eastern white cedar for the building of boats.
When Jacques Cartier discovered Quebec,
               on the advice of the Aboriginals
he used cedar to cure scurvy.

By the bridge I noticed a pool
bordered by slates of shale,
reminding me of the eye's pupil
               a kaleidoscope
of blues, browns, and charcoals,
breaking the surface, forming circles
which radiate through other circles
into precise patterns.

This morning at the coffee takeout,
the waitress spoke through the loudspeaker
about the terrible rainy day,
and when I said the sun shines within,
her laughter rippled through the air.

Reflections On My Writing Desk

I push my keyboard away.
In the reflection on my writing desk
I see a person.
I recognize the lines around his mouth,
the shape of lips,
the outlines of cheeks.
The glass on my oval desk
has become a mirror.
When I was eight
I placed a wood-framed mirror on the floor
and entered it as Alice did,
stepping through the looking glass.
My world was turned upside down
as another reality.
I was flying and the objects around me
slowly rose toward the night sky,
pushing through one cosmic frame after another.
My mind could travel out of itself.
Then I was back
looking at the reflection of lights
of the passing cars on Weston Road
beaming on the room's ceiling.
Now as I look at myself
I think of that child,
the glass case mirroring me—
this older man travelling through time.

Resonance

1

Sometimes all I have to do
is close my eyes
to remember the past.
The sound of the sea,
the way the waves crash on the rocks,
the sky turning dark, the curlews calling out
to each other over the distant white caps,
the moon shining over the North Sea.

I can see my father standing
on the turret with me.
We begin the slow descent,
down to the moat, out the small door
where an old wise man,
the castle keeper, stands
holding in one hand a small red horseshoe,
with the other he draws a small metal ball.
"Watch this."
The silver ball flies to the horseshoe.
"That's magic."

2

I only have to close my eyes
to hear the power of my thoughts.
I remember early Sunday
standing on the railway crossing with my father,
waiting for the train to Belfast
and feeling a warm mist steaming
through the woody smell of ties,
the oil glowing in blue and purple splotches
mixed with the sea's scent.
The railway tracks curve toward the horizon,
following the shape of hills.

The Castle

I'm in a castle with many rooms
that I cannot escape.
I slide a false bookcase in the wall,
step into the ornate library from the Victorian age:
the ladies at Cheltenham ready for the steeplechase,
young women corseted in servitude,
lords standing over the spread tiger.
Above a stone horse surveys all
with a cold eye.

From outside the history of family is a picture book,
inside the broken relics of the past:
a stranded unicorn
and a deserted princess on the wall.
The books lie in heaps
with stained pages and blurred print.
The rooms grow large and multiply
with the year's passage.
I'm trapped.
Where is the door
that will lead me out
into the fresh air of night?

Toward Tory Island

The ferry leaves the mainland,
heading out into the Atlantic—
the way fishermen who could read the waves
have travelled for centuries
in the systole and diastole of the sea.

The island emerges on the horizon
like a whale's long tapered back
with a mica tower—an enigmatic god
of Easter Island.
Deep within the island's dark night
sleeps Balor, god of evil,
and his grandson, Lugh who vanquished him.

On the island I hear Gaelic in the waves,
a tongue that flourished for a thousand years.
The loving, dipping rhythms,
the rising and falling of vowels
beyond the conqueror's sword.

On his long journey from the oak groves of Derry
Colmcille landed here in the 6th century
and crowned Duggan the first Tory king.
Since that time they have had kings.
I expected to see him,
a tall man with a hat,
greeting people.

He arrives on his red Geleni motorbike.
"Are there any O'Briens on Tory Island?"
"Aye, there is O'Briens"
and traces them back to Meenaclady.

I follow the deserted streets
with overgrown gardens,
weathered houses leaning together
against the constant threat of wind and water.
Did my great-grandmother Annie O'Brien
stroll among these streets
in the mid nineteenth century?

I walk toward the island's eastern end.
There is nothing but the sound of sea
and one tree growing before the priest's house.

I see among the ruins
a torpedo shaped cylinder standing on its edge,
in the centre of nowhere,
a sentinel staring to the North Atlantic.
Here, bored teens drive wrecked cars
to the rock face, push them over.
One night a chassis gets hooked by the cliff,
and still hangs there precariously.

I return to the tower of Toraigh,
standing by the sea as a pinnacle against the sky.
Still the fishermen lean their nets and gear here.
A weathered disk tries to bring
the world on its satellite waves.
I pass the wandering dogs
and strutting of afternoon cocks,
to the graveyard by the old Celtic tower.

Walking the Dead

Since the 10th century
the people have brought the dead here.
They carried them from Tory Island
in the humming procession
to the spirit place.

They wrapped and carried them
through the pillared gate,
up the hill
toward the mound
where you can see
the land and the long line walking the dead.

They carried them as those around
would later carry each other,
and they laid them under great slabs
in the resting beds of their ancestors.

In a misty morning
warm enough to open the earth
I stand in the circle of tombstones
looking at ewes and lambs
moving slowly
as they graze among the gravestones.

The House of Mary Coyle

The last time I was here
Mary showed me her house,
a room filled with tumbled furniture,
shelves lined with Irish books,
old tobacco cans and tea tins.
Fire glowed in the embers,
Irish Times piled around the hearth
with ornamental angels.

On the wall was a faded painting of Londonderry spires
and a portrait of Jesus with the sacred heart.

She knew the Gaelic
and quoted a poem about the last chieftain, Cahir O'Doherty
who once ruled these lands from his castle.

She mentioned her relatives,
a professor of nuclear physics in Geneva
and a man who invented the game, *The Weakest Link.*

She had an intelligent cast of eye,
fine lines on her face;
her voice had a melody of water
flowing through rocks.

When I asked her to stand for a photograph
she insisted upon putting on lipstick.

The white house is abandoned now,
the barn is crumbling.
The overhanging branches of the apple tree
have been cut by the landlord
in order to watch for robbers,
although there is not much to steal.

Anne Frank House

The streets of Amsterdam are quiet.
The cool sun gleams on dark canal water.
I'm in a long line with others
waiting to enter the house of Anne Frank.
Someone talks about discovering a relative in Jerusalem,
two American girls are complaining about time change.
They do not seem fully awake this morning.

The first room is bare.
This is the way Otto Frank left it.
I imagine Anne living here day after day,
hiding from the outside world.
The window curtain blind with fear.

It is not known who betrayed them.
One day the German truck with soldiers arrived
and opened the bookcase door.
They were transported to Westerbork,
then to Auschwitz.
She died one month before liberation.

I am alone in her room
in a state of dreaming.

The walls are full of young voices from the past
whispering their secrets at night.

Through the window I see the garden,
the church bells are ringing loudly at midday.

Escape to Siberia

Under the hut's palm leaves
at VIK resort in Punta Cana
the rain begins,
and Shifra starts talking about June 1941,
"Father awoke us whispering to my mother:
'Go as far from here as you can.'
Soon we were on our way to the station
in a rickety taxi through the old streets of Liepaja,
with my brother and younger sister.
My mother was pregnant.
For days the train was moving away
from Latvia, deeper into Russia.
One evening German planes dropped bombs
on the train.
It stopped, only our car wasn't hit.
The people crowded into it
and the train lunged onward.
But it broke down again. We walked to the next station.
It seemed the path would never end,
just kept stretching, an uncertain promise
through fallen branches, the sharp rocks.
Sleeping under the trees,
we heard the howling of wolves,
the prowling of night animals,
lightning flashed from distant bombing.
My shoes wore out.
I had to walk barefoot.
My younger sister cried. I cried too.

I was only five years old.
We were hungry.
Sometimes a convoy of Russian soldiers
threw us stale loaves, packages of biscuits.
Finally we saw the tower's red station, Velikiye Luki.
The stationmaster asked Mother where she wanted to go.

'We are going to Siberia.'
In Tyumen we were put up in an orphanage.
Because Mother was pregnant we all survived.
When the war ended,
we returned to Liepaja.
The city in ruins, our house rubble, relatives gone.
Later I found out that Father was a KGB officer
and was killed the day after we left."

Drops fall from palm leaves.
The rain has ended.

Opa's Zuider Zee Painting

He had bought this valuable
19th century Schotel painting
at a local auction for 700 *gulden,*
depicting a storm on the Zuider Zee.

It was not only a painting
but an allegory of Opa's life at sea,
reminding him of that night under a darkening sky,
the wind thrashing the sails,
the water breaking over the bow.

He was close enough to see
another boat listing badly,
a family calling for help.
With a giant sweep of waves, the sails disappeared.
He saw two men waving their hands,
heard their cries and steered toward them
but there was only the sea.

He no longer knew the time.
Holding the wheel,
guided only by his instinct
he was navigating the waves.
Then the sky broke open,
the sea calmed.
Haarlem was near.

Now, as his family sat around the table during wartime,
trying to forget hunger,
he knew what had to be done.

Soon two men came to the door.
He lifted the painting off the hook
and carried it away.

"Thank you, Meneer Veldhuisen."
He covered the Schotel, carrying it away.
Opa's youngest daughter saw her father staring
for a long time at the empty wall.
By the door was an unmarked sack of flour.

Dan

"I was picked up in the railway station.
and then sent to Amsfoort.
Dutch men between 16 and 45
had to go to work in Germany."

"They put a mark on our uniforms:
a black circle if you were in the black market,
an orange circle, if you were in politics,
a pink circle if you were gay.
I got a green mark because they thought I was a criminal."

"I worked in the blacksmith shop
repairing horseshoes, belts and buckles for SS officers.
The prisoners rested when they were shitting.
If we stayed too long in the toilet they beat us."

"I was hungry. I was hungry.
We all had to use the same barrel in the barrack.
I got dysentery. I was dying.
The priest, a prisoner, gave me the last rites.
My faith pulled me through."

"I Was in the Warsaw Uprising"

On the celebration of Poland Independence Day
we gather at the Ontario Legislature.
In a room decorated by paintings of Inuit artists
I noticed an older man with an armband.
"What does it signify?" I ask him.
"I fought in the Warsaw Uprising."

He was thirteen, a messenger, carrying important notes
from building to building.
He had a gun, six bullets and three hand grenades.
He was a boy fighting a man's war,
trying to save his city.

Around him Warsaw continues to be destroyed.
The Jewish ghetto burned,
the flames engulfed the synagogues,
the markets, century old-houses.
He heard the people scream
and remembered a Jewish girl
trying to escape by climbing the wire
shot by a German soldier.

During battle, the enemy artillery pierced his leg.
He spent months in a hospital, recovering.
"I was taken to a house with younger army boys.
The basement room was crowded,
boys were fighting for a spot.
A tall guard boy told me to sleep against the wall.
"I was so tired.
I closed my eyes to forget the war
when a sixteen-year-old boy approached me."
'We will play a game.

You must guess what hand
I have placed the bullet in.
If you win, you can keep this place ...'

"I chose the right one. It was empty."
He took my place.
In a few minutes the bombing began.
Our house was hit. The roof collapsed,
the smoke filled the room.
I felt the weight of his dead body against mine.

I spent some time in a German prison camp.
I still remember it as if it were yesterday."
He picks up his cup
the coffee's fresh smell rises.

Yellow Star

Sitting across the table, I noticed
the cellophane package.
The crinkled plastic,
not quite clear,
contained something almost alive.
I took it out of the bag.
It was the star of David
which belonged to my Aunt Fenna's father,
identifying him as a Jew.
He was sent to a work camp for resettlement.

Video World

Tempted by light, colour & music,
I enter the video game room.
Great action, real figures,
compelling graphics, high colour resolution.
Cartoon super heroes fight gangsters.
INSERT COIN.
Men pump quarters into the slots of their desires.
INSERT COIN.
Women dance slowly across the screen.
Lonely men smile.
Pale-faced Madonnas drift through mirages.
INSERT ANOTHER COIN
Reckless hockey players bang pucks—
sudden death without penalty.
INSERT COIN.
This is a war theatre.
A young sniper leans toward the enemy.
Soldiers shoot at him, at you.
"Shoot them. Kill them."
The machine screams—flashes its guns.
Good. They're dead.
A man explodes on a bloodless screen.

These are the wars we fight here,
spending money to keep the machine running.
Outside war is not a game.

Terra Incognita

after the painting "Kompozycja" 2012 by Rapsa

There are paintings that emerge from the world.
You can peer into the blue
that sends you into the cosmos
to see forms that you recognize
as the verdant isthmus or the textured Pyrenees.

You visualize it as the geography,
decipher the map's legends.
Perhaps you can see the terracotta of Tuscany
or wildfires burning over
the grey earth's basalt,
inviting you to go deeper into this terra incognita,

to feel the force of earth
in the palimpsest of weather.
The white mist
unfurling from the unconsciousness,
the unexplained natural birth of colour in landforms,
ah … the artwork of imagination.

Fox Playing in Early Twilight

He was suddenly here
gnawing on a green apple, trying
trying to get his teeth into its skin.

The apple rolled away,
bounced through the grass
as he jumped,
seeking to control it,
a cat chasing a ball of thread,
leaping through the air.

He was moving toward us,
giving up and letting the apple nestle
in the grey dusk's grass.

This cagey hunter
stirring the dust,
snapping at crickets

caught us in his play.

Algonquin Logger's Chute

After Simcoe's last Yonge Street portage's vertigo,
     the wandering rocks, the shifting shoulder blade,
the throbbing yoke,
     we emerge with canoe before dark green lagoon
of strewn graveyard of trees,
        twisted in all shapes and sizes
     to step out into
Hieronymus Bosch's beach party

and joke about this place as the antipode to "Club Med":
        "masochists anonymous"
in Procruste's Holiday Inn:
        "We'll take good care of you,
        stretch you until you're in fine shape."

Everywhere bones:
     tender clavicle, slender humerus, jagged ribs,
        warped tibia, fractured femur; the pelvis's girdle
      shimmers in the last quiver of pleasure. And the sockets
in Yorick's funhouse, survey it all,
       taking it all in, taking it all down.

To get clear of this ghostly carnival of the animals
      with no Virgil to be your guide
        in this broken down honky-tonk town.
You have to act out this labyrinthian fantasy
      where the minotaur is not the beast, but the mind.

First Spring Walk in the Mountains

The valley is filled with light and shadows,
yet awakening from winter snows.
Already in May the mosquitoes
create a huzza around me.

There is nothing in this half of the world—
only mountains, forests, and ravens.
Why do the trees change me and
make me breathe in a different way?

The path opens up
and the earth's stones
assume the various shapes of jewels.
Dead trees are abandoned candelabras.

Here, I breathe the land,
pure ozone, blossom scents, damp moss.
To love the land you have to see it,
go beyond yourself.
You have to love cold,
fires at night, lonely snow,
and to see in spring slender forms of dandelions
as a row of ballet dancers in a Degas painting.

Each individual thing speaks out of itself.
Take it and hold it
until you hear the rocks sing.

The Night Has a Clear Sanity About It

I step into the street
silver strands of snow
are weaving the bare pavement.

The wind blows coldly against me,
the night has a clear sanity about it.

I watch the barman talking to the last waiter
(he looks like my father).
On the pale restaurant walls the vine leaves
conceal South Sea lovers.

Someone lights up a cigarette.
Trees reach beyond violet lamps near
the shell station—a deserted adobe,
a truck rushes beneath the underpass.

The wind blows coldly against me,
the night has a clear sanity about it.

Against the stars a tarpaulin flaps.
Frayed political posters and movie ads are faded,
a child's finger painting emerges from the garbage.
Beyond a black church the crystal moon drifts.

We Are Always Searching for a Place

We keep going back to the beginning
to the larger element as if origins could explain
the matrix of our being
(the source of stars, the Eagle's Nest,
the nuclei dance.)

We keep searching for the stories
the intricate rhythms of ancestors' songs
looking beyond the constellations.
The myths are being played out
until we find the strands of thought
love in the voice of many-tongued words
in the midst of chaos
trying not to forget the place where we grew up.
Carrying our ancestors' original vision,
clarity of their maps within our genes
encoded now—we grasp.

Fire and Water
(2020)

Song for Kochanie

I want you to be as eccentric as a seahorse
curvaceous as a mermaid
secret as ancient amber.

Eva, my words are searching for you
I imagine you walking along twilight sands
and I follow the path
my daring artist, poet, mischievous rebel.
Tell me who you are when in the darkness
I feel the lightness of your being
opening my lips to pleasure.

Wild maiden
let our bed become
a boat rocking in the waves.

Absence

Absence is a cold snow suspended beyond the window,
returning to an empty house with so many rooms, alone.
It is waking up in a bed expecting someone beside you.
Absence is a white page that does not want to be written on
or a white canvas which does not invite shapes and colour.
Absence is a pale moon which no longer reflects your desire.
But absence is the country where we are nourished by memory's river,
which makes us conscious of each other.
Absence is the discovery of treasure.

Listen to the Sea

You make me read nature
as only you can—
how the sea mirrors the waves
on the border of darkness
when the water is darker than the sky
with only a band of blue.
To see the beach in a seismograph of light
and how the waves moving back to the sea
leave a line in the sand—the little hills of music.

Eva in the Duinoord Hotel

This photo becomes a Vermeer painting.
You are placed carefully against the light
which peeks through the window
in a blurred green tone.
The world is framed.
The tablecloth is spreading the light
so evenly, folded with shadows.
The silver curved glasses form the air.
You sit before me in this black veiled dress,
and look into me, lady of my heart.

In the Forest

I was standing at the beginning of an enchanted forest, textures and leaves composed like a tapestry. The path seemed to rise through the trees into the sky. I had to take this path as a spiritual adventure. Suddenly I saw a woman at my side, wearing a white dress. She had radiance about her. The light fell on her. It seemed the light was raining on her. We were destined to take this path together. She stood there waiting.

Acknowledgements

The poems in this book have been previously published in the following magazines and anthologies: *An Amazing Eclectic Anthology*, *The Antigonish Review*, *The Artis*, *Body Language: A Head-to-Toe Anthology*, *Bywords*, *The Canadian Author*, *Canadian Literature*, *The Cormorant*, *Cross/cut: Contemporary Quebec Poetry*, *CVII*, *ellipse*, *The Emery Village Voice*, *The Fiddlehead*, *Folio*, *Following the Plough*, *Garden Varieties*, *The Greenfield Review*, *The Honest Ulsterman*, *Landmarks: An Anthology of New Atlantic Canadian Poetry*, *The Lyric Paragraph*, *Matrix*, *Montreal English Poetry of the Seventies*, *Montreal Writers' Forum*, *The Nashwaak Review*, *The New Brunswick Reader*, *Odra*, *PoetryMagazine.Com*, *Poetry Toronto*, *Pottersfield Portfolio*, *Prism International*, *Quarry*, *Storm Warning 2*, *Stuffed Crocodile*, *That Sign of Perfection*, *Under the Mulberry Tree*, *Versus*, *Waves*, *Wayzegoose*, *Windsor Review*, *Zymergy*.

First of all, I would like to thank my wife, Eva Kolacz, for masterfully editing this manuscript and for her dedication and love. Special thanks go to Peter Midgley for excellent copy-editing and to Gary Geddes for reading the manuscript and making valuable suggestions. And I am indebted to my publisher, Michael Mirolla, Guernica Editions.

I would like to express my thanks to the Faculté des études supérieures et de la recherche of the Université de Moncton for creation grants, and the Département Arts et lettres, Université de Moncton, Campus d'Edmundston. I would like to acknowledge the financial support of Alberta Arts Culture, the Canada Council and the New Brunswick Arts Board. I would like to express my gratitude to the publishers of my books: Clark Leverett of Killaly Press; Louis Dudek at DC Books; John MacCauley with Maker Press; and Heather Ferguson at Agawa Press. I would especially like to express my gratitude to Marty Gervais at Black Moss Press, and to Antonio D'Alfonso at Guernica Editions.

I would also like to thank my friends, Brian Bartlett, Samira Belyazid, René Blais, Anne Cimon, Steven De Gama, Rolf Harvey, Charlotte Hussey, Paul Hedeen, Bruce Hunter, Les Kelly, Tim Lambrinos, John B. Lee, Adrian King-Edwards, Vicky Lentz, Bruce Meyer, James Reaney,

Colleen Thibaudeau, Réjean Toussaint, and Bill Willan for their encouragement and support over the years. And I would like to thank my good friends from Montreal, Stephen Morrissey and Carolyn Zonailo. A special thanks to my professors—Arthur Barker, Henry Beissel, Clark Blaise, Gary Geddes, Don Hensley, Hugh Hood, William Kinsley, Ninian Mellamphy and Philip Stratford.

I would like to thank my parents and my sisters, Eleanor, Roberta, Wendy, Kelly and my step daughter, Patty for their support, as well as my extraordinary children, Sean and Emma.

About the Author

LAURENCE HUTCHMAN was born in Belfast, Northern Ireland, and grew up in Toronto. He received his PhD from the Université de Montreal and has taught at several universities. For twenty-three years he was a professor of English literature at the Université de Moncton at the Edmundston Campus. Hutchman has published 12 books of poetry, co-edited the anthology *Coastlines: the Poetry of Atlantic Canada* and edited *In the Writers' Words*. His poetry has received many grants and awards, including the Alden Nowlan Award for Excellence and has been translated into numerous languages. In 2017 he was named poet laureate of Emery, north Toronto. He lives with his wife, the artist and poet Eva Kolacz, in Oakville, Ontario.

Printed in August 2020
by Gauvin Press,
Gatineau, Québec